HUMANISING THE WORKPLACE

Humanising the Workplace

NEW PROPOSALS AND PERSPECTIVES

EDITED BY
RICHARD N. OTTAWAY

CROOM HELM LONDON

© 1977 Richard N. Ottaway
Croom Helm Ltd, 2-10 St John's Road, London SW11
British Library Cataloguing in Publication Data

Humanising the work place.
   1. Job Satisfaction
   I. Ottaway, Richard N
   658.31'42   HF5549.5.J63

ISBN 0-85664-345-9

Printed in Great Britain by Biddles Ltd, Guildford, Surrey

This book is dedicated to

BOB MARSHALL

and all who try to humanise the work place

CONTENTS

Preface

1. An Apology For Change *Richard N. Ottaway* — 13
2. Technological Determinism *John Langrish* — 25
3. Are Computer Systems and Humanised Work Compatible? *Mary Weir* — 44
4. Taylor in the Office *Michael J.E. Cooley* — 65
5. Worker Education For Industrial Democracy *W. Wilson and J.B. Nichol* — 78
6. Alienation in the Workplace: A Transactional Analysis Approach *Mary Cox and Charles Cox* — 101
7. Management Education Methods for Humanising the Workplace *Cary L. Cooper* — 123
8. New Management Attitudes to the Humanisation of Work *J.N. Watson* — 135
9. Democratising the Workplace *Ernie Roberts* — 149
10. The State of the Unions *Mick Rice* — 158

Index — 172

CONTRIBUTORS

Richard N. Ottaway, lecturer in management sciences, University of Manchester Institute of Science and Technology.

John Langrish, senior lecturer in management sciences, University of Manchester Institute of Science and Technology.

Mary Weir, research fellow, Manchester Business School.

Michael J.E. Cooley, senior design engineer, Lucas Aerospace.

W. Wilson, principal lecturer in industrial relations, Stocksbridge College.

J.B. Nichol, lecturer in adult education, University of Manchester.

Mary Cox, management consultant.

Charles Cox, lecturer in management sciences, University of Manchester Institute of Science and Technology.

Cary L. Cooper, professor of management education methods, University of Manchester Institute of Science and Technology.

J.N. Watson, head of personnel development division, Shell International Petroleum Company, Limited.

Ernie Roberts, assistant general secretary, AUEW, Engineering Section.

Mick Rice, shop steward, Lucas Starter Factory.

PREFACE

This volume is a collection of commissioned papers offering new perspectives and proposals for humanising the work place. From the dawn of the industrial revolution to the present time, students, trade unionists, workers, managers, and theoreticians have struggled with a series of problems related to work. In the early days, pulling together raw materials, manpower, capital and technology was the uppermost problem. Later, around the turn of this century, organising these same ingredients under the influence of science and in the face of the world markets was the problem. During the ensuing years developing technologies for predictable, cheap production coupled with resolving conflicts of equitable work arrangements have been important.

Today, many of these basic issues have been laid to rest. Now the skills of capitalising, engineering and marketing are of such potency that we dare ask questions about the value of the whole process. We struggle with issues that our forefathers would have thought luxurious. One of these large, complex areas of inquiry on our agenda today is how to humanise the work place.

Why *humanising* the work place for the title? Using the word humanising is an attempt to find a word which avoids the usual connotations associated with various words used around the world to describe the same phenomena. For instance, one tends to associate self-management with Yugoslavia, co-determination with West Germany and industrial democracy with Norway. Job satisfaction and worker participation seem to be used more widely in the United States and Great Britain. Humanising the work place is the title chosen to embrace a wide spectrum of issues, concepts, and aspects of all efforts to have work enhance human beings.

The study of humanising the work place is a soft field. There are few track records, success stories, or guides for management, trade unionists, or social scientists. This book is not intended to offer solutions nor give guidelines on how to humanise the work place. Rather this is a collection of explorations of the issues at stake. Each chapter works on part of the puzzle. Consequently, the book does not present a unified argument. The authors are in agreement on the values underlying their thinking and their commitment to working for a humanised work place.

The chapters reflect a diversity of viewpoints. *Ottaway* gives background thinking for considering organisational change. Technological determinism is explored by *Langrish* who feels we are at a break point in history. *Weir* discusses how computers are both for and against humanised work. *Cooley* warns that F.W. Taylor and scientific management is moving beyond the shop floor to the technical and administrative quarters. New worker education is hypothesised by *Wilson* and *Nichol* based on the work of Freire. *Cox* and *Cox* give a perspective on alienation from transactional analysis. How management education methods will be affected by humanisation is the topic addressed by *Cooper*. *Watson* discusses the new management attitudes emerging and required for the future. The role of unions is proposed by *Roberts*. Some of the problems that unions experience are described and discussed by *Rice*.

Our aim is to treat the phenomena on a conceptual level which can be read through the eyes of any of the more specific efforts to humanise the work place. Our hope is to present thinking that is apolitical and acultural. We forward our perspectives and proposals from the university and the work place to stimulate the inquiry of how to humanise the work place — how to conceptualise and implement a new norm of working together that meets the needs of the workers of all levels and the goals of modern organisations.

Richard N. Ottaway

1 AN APOLOGY FOR CHANGE

Richard N. Ottaway

Introduction

Professor Jovan Djordjevic, speaking at the University of Belgrade last summer, said that words such as romance, justice, democracy, self-management, are words that change one's life. By this he meant that Yugoslav self-management does not mean merely distributing the wealth differently nor inviting workers to make decisions alongside of managers. Worker participation, industrial democracy, self-management, whatever term is used to mean humanising the work place, is not just a re-arrangement of work roles, decision-making procedures, or re-distribution of wealth. Humanising the work place means, for most work places, a new way of life based on a new value system of working together in an open, sharing, learning, responsible, and rewarding way.

To work together in a new way requires radical change. The point of this chapter is to make an apology for change. The classical meaning of an apology is "A defence or explanation of one's position in a language that the adversary can understand" (Richardson 1947). My definition of an apology is an advocate's explanation of a phenomenon directed to a resistant audience in a language understood by both. I hope that proves to be a good description of this chapter. I intend it to be an explanation of change from my viewpoint, as an advocate of change professionally engaged in the study and implementation of it. I feel that members of work organisations may benefit from an apology to legitimate change as a natural aspect of the work place.

Members of work organisations have many reasons to be afraid of change. The hope of this apology is that a few of these fears may be reduced. My first point is on the inadequacy of the current change technology. We are just beginning to consider change a social function worthy of special study in the social sciences. Next some effort is devoted to answering the question of why change is important under the title 'Change is Learning'. Following that the issue of cultural values as obstacles to change is explored from two perspectives: American and British values. And lastly, another approach to exploring obstacles is the suggestion that there may be an unconscious collusion between the organisations who say they want to change and those who step forward

13

to be helpful as change agents.

Knowledge of change in its infancy

Our knowledge about change is primitive. Primitive in that it lacks a developed language, for example. Many of the words in the literature are confusing. What, for example, is that period of time called when an organisation is undergoing a change? Is it a change process, a change programme, a change procedure? All of those terms will appear interchangeably in the literature.

On the other hand, whereas the time while change is occuring has several names, there are a number of aspects of organisational change which have no name. There is no widely used verb meaning organisational change. The current change literature contains a wide variety of phrases such as: change taking place, creating change, implementing change, change being effected, bringing about change, and changing the organisation.

More subtle and more illustrative of the plight of the change agent (a questionable word) and the changee (a new word) communicating on the subject is the fact that no word is in common usage among social scientists, practitioners, or organisation members to describe an organisation in its degree of readiness to change, state of imminence of change, or when that change period is over, complete, happened, or not any longer in that nameless state of change happening.

The dictionary lists change as a verb, a noun, and an adjective. The reader and the apologist will have problems with language. Should one use change as a verb? That would mean using 'changing the organisation' type statements which sounds very pro-active and implies that change can be activated or set into motion. Using change as a verb suggests that change happens at will and removes it from being out of our control. The deterministic nature of change, which is often seen as threatening the comfortable structures we have created for ourselves, is reduced when using change as a verb.

Should we use change as a noun? That would be using 'bringing about change' type statements. The noun usage might imply that change does have powers of its own. Nouns need verbs. They require action to come to them. Using change as a noun gives the impression of it standing on its own and our having to do something to it. There has been an experience in each of our lives which says that change is on its own course and we have very little control over it.

The assumption in this apology is that such an attitude about change is due mainly to our limited knowledge of change. The powers we

An Apology for Change

ascribe to change grow out of our anxiety over our ability to cope with change. Consequently, further study and more practice at changing organisations will reduce our anxieties and change will come more into our control. If that should be the case, in the future we can look for change to be used less as a noun and more as a verb.

In the past few decades a field of practice has grown up among behavioural scientists devoted to implementing organisational change. It is called organisation development (see Watson chapter). This newly found branch of applied behavioural sciences traces its family from sociology and social psychology. Kahn (1974) offers his critique of this field, which supports the argument here that the practice of changing organisations is in its infancy. He can only point to three organisation development research reports which satisfy his classical research criteria: Coch and French (1948) and their work on the effects of participation; Morse and Reimer (1956) and their work on satisfaction as related to decision-making; and Trist and Bamforth (1951) and their work on the socio-technic concept.

Across the country their are several degree courses being offered in the area of organisational change or organisation development. Short courses for special skills in change seem to be increasing. But as yet not many firms list organisation development in their personnel job descriptions. There is a professional organisation with about 175 members (OD Network). Only a small number of them are overtly charged to work on change. The subject is in its infancy and has the usual problems of a developing field of study and practice.

Changing is learning

Managers will often ask if I believe in change for the sake of change. The answer is basically no. As a matter of fact, I do not think that change for the sake of change exists. I think it is a myth about change that appears when our anxieties about change rise.

There are two reasons why I do not think that change for the sake of change exists. The first is that I think that change as an activity is a form of learning. While engaged in the act of changing one is actually learning many new behaviours. Learning is also changing one's self. Katz and Kahn (1966) think that we can safely transfer insights about individual behaviour to organisational behaviour. Assuming that they are right, I think that the work of Rogers (1951, 1969) on learning has application to changing organisations. He has stated that one only learns that which is in one's own self-interest. That is, someone only learns that which they feel they need to learn when they feel they need to learn it. This is known as the 'felt-need' theory. It is an easy step to translate this into the change situation, if we agree that changing is a form of learning, and say that individuals and organisations only change their behaviour when it meets a felt need in them. That is to say, that which appears to be change for the sake of change is more than likely change taking place because it meets a felt need in a person or organisation.

Now the question comes up, if an organisation is changing, does that mean that all the persons in that organisation feel that need to change? The answer is basically no. Organisations do not change by unanimously voting to do so. They change dynamically, or politically, when it feels safe and in the self-interest of those with the power to change it. Usually a few, or many, in the organisation do not feel the need. I think that it is those who do not feel the need to change, but are forced to change anyway, that will say that change is for the sake of change.

We might conclude from the foregoing argument that those involved in deciding the change will tend not to think that the change is for the sake of change while those excluded from the decisions about change may think that change is for the sake of change. This in itself is a crucial point about how to increase the chances of successfully changing the behaviour of an organisation. Coch and French (1948) were the first to give some empirical data on the notion that those involved in planning a change are less resistant to the change. With an experiment in the garment industry they found that there was less resistance to change among those more involved in the decisions about that change. From this kind of evidence, many change agents follow the practice of involving those who are going to change in the planning of the change. (Jones 1969).

Up until now the discussion has moved along on the assumption that change is voluntary. When we consider the same questions in a situation where change is forced the answers are even more convincing. Most of the change we experience is forced on us. We rarely have the opportunity to actively consent or reject the change that we experience. The changes that we experience are meeting the felt need of someone else; such as, parents, teachers, bosses, creditors and the like. Even forced change is not change for the sake of change. It meets the needs of the enforcer.

Change is not senseless, unpredictable, unaccountable behaviour to be feared. It can be understood. Humanising the work place might be said to be an effort to establish a work place where people are involved in deciding their own change based on their own felt needs.

An Apology for Change

Yet, the answer is not an unqualified no. There is some reasonable defence for changing for the sake of change. For instance, the act of changing does increase our skills for changing. Some organisations move their personnel around and offer career patterns that reward one for changing their skills. Some organisations also use training schemes which require their members to be in new learning situations from time to time (see the chapters by Wilson and Nichol as well as Cooper). These organisations might well be thought of as increasing their change skills. In this sense change for the sake of change, or learning for the sake of learning, appears to be valuable. Such behaviour in an organisation does imply, at least, that learning (changing) is valuable and is endorsed by the culture of the organisation.

The conclusion might be drawn, therefore, that such organisations can change with greater ease. They can include more people in the change process who have helpful skills. And there will be less fear of change for the sake of change. Also, the organisation with practice at changing can respond more creatively to forced change when it occurs. Fundamentally, the organisation which practises changing will have skills for changing; like those who practise learning have skills for learning.

Is organisational change Americanisation?

Stephen Spender (1974, p. 28) says that '*Americanization*, the process of *Americanizing*, is the shadow of a future in which the world becomes America. For Europeans, the deepest fear is of the dissolution of European methods and ways of thinking, and of the European past, into the American present.' This issue needs to be explored in an apology for change because so much of the technology of organisational change comes from America. As an American teaching organisational change in Great Britain, I often feel a reticence, and sometimes a hostility, to the subject by British managers and students. They quickly notice that the book lists are dominated by American authors.

The reason there are so many American authors on organisational change is because they have made this their special subject. Spender's thoughts would easily interpret this American activity as part of their culture. Spender thinks of the Europeans and Americans in objective/subjective contrast. He equates Europe with the objective. This means that the Europeans think of themselves in objective language such as in terms of their tradition. About the English he says, 'The English have the sense of moving along a continuous line. They may go back along the line to a livelier past, but they do not have the feeling of several lines available to them.'

Spender equates America with the subjective. By that term he means that the American's need to find out for himself is his form of self-expression. In keeping with the above, he would see the Americans as feeling that there are several lines open to them. The American feels compelled to find the best line which may even require frequently shifting from line to line. The American can become frantic with this openness and lack of past. All the American drive is for the future which is seen as a limitless reserve of lines all leading to something better than the moment. Whereas tradition is the key descriptive word for Europe, the American Dream, and all it implies of better, unknown, yet to come, an omen to follow, is the key descriptive phrase for America.

There appears to be a conflict between the value of the known as it is seen in the present or the past (as the British would see it) and the value of changing to something better, which is almost anything other than what we have in the present, from the past (as the Americans would see it). The conclusion often drawn from this conflict is that the Americans are for progress at any cost while the British know the cost and are keeping the better life rooted in the past.

As an apologist in this argument, my suggestion is that we see both of these positions as caricatures in the sense that if America and Great Britain could live as they wish in isolation they might live something like this. But the truth is that both of them are forced to interact with each other, and with many other values in the world. Therefore, it is not helpful to try to resolve this problem on these grounds. Two points might be helpful in releasing organisational change from the Ugly American catalogue and make it available for consideration in its own right. The first of these points is that the Americans have the American Dream not because they objectively select to do so. Rather, they have it because it meets a need in them. No one else has to be threatened by them and their need to study, practise, theorise, and experiment with change all the time. Let the American's need to understand change be his contribution to other cultures.

The second point which might facilitate release from seeing organisational change as Americanisation is seeing change as an aspect of life rather than as progress. Organisational change, because of its American heritage, does get labelled as progress. And many rightful questions can be asked whether it is progress or not. I have found viewing change as learning helpful. Learning is a natural aspect of life in both cultures and therefore that may be a good common ground to use to escape from the

An Apology for Change

fruitless argument about Americanisation.

Can organisational change take place in British culture?

As a result of discussions in London with organisation development consultants, Steele (1976) has offered seven assumptions usually held by such practitioners. He also suggests that cultural factors may block effective implementation of change in Great Britain. The seven assumptions are:

- Doing better is a good thing. It is worth the effort to improve the effectiveness of an organisation.
- The facts are friendly. In the long run it is better to deal with the reality of the situation and the facts will help to do so.
- People should have a personal ownership of their own life space. Everyone has the right to influence those decisions that impact on their life experience.
- A changing environment requires the system to be adaptive in terms of its structure and process. There is no perfect organisational form; rather organisations must have the ability to adapt, reshape, and to change.
- Change does not have to be haphazard. Organisations have some choices available about their future as long as they are pro-active in planning the future rather than reactive in acceptance of stimuli for change.
- The results of change actions are not always wholly predictable and controllable. Although it is possible to initiate change rather than wait for it to happen, it is not always possible to have perfect information, in advance, about all the consequences of that change.
- Behavioural science knowledge can contribute to organisational health. We can apply behavioural science concepts to problems of organisational development.

Steele found in his discussions that there are some very strong blocks to these assumptions. The cultural value of one's style (how one lives, works and plays) is as important as how effective one is. The form of the organisation and having a fixed method to cope with stimuli seems to be more important than whether the form or method is effective or not.

Personal form also is important. Politeness might actually stand in the way of exposing uncomfortable facts about an organisation. Many facts are protected from exposure by law. One thinks of the financial status of the firm and the Secrets Act of the Government as examples.

In British culture there is a tendency to think that some people are capable of managing their own lives and the lives of others, such as their subordinates. It is a widely held value in Britain that by the time someone is in a management position, they deserve to be there. The separate school systems for managers and workers, generally speaking, might keep this going. Comprehensive schools may be challenging this value.

Many of the values that might block change stem from the high value placed on rational behaviour. Problems associated with change such as predictability and the scientificness of change technology are often a defence tactic in order not to have to accept the control of change. The major point I want to make in this apology is that change can take place in a predictable manner with those changing also controlling the pace and degree of change. Primitive as our change technology is, it is not to be completely discounted as irrational.

The real issue at stake on the rationality point, in my opinion, is the issue of taking up a pro-active management of change in one's self-interest as compared to re-active management to protect one from being swept into an out-of-control change. The out-of-control change is a myth. Re-active management is change out-of-control. The roots of re-active management are deep in the British value system. It is the strong strain of fatalism in Great Britain which misleads many into thinking that the height of management skill is making the best out of the bad situation.

Steele's findings from his discussions might be said to be that British organisations are going to be slow to accept organisational change as a reality for three reasons: it is too risky, it is too irrational and it is not like us. Steele is pessimistic about the possibilities of organisational change of the OD type in Great Britain.

A couple of ideas come to mind in response to reading Steele. One is that organisations that do not want to be changed, cannot be changed, except by force. Once we conclude that the British value system blocks much chance of change, then the kind of statements that Professor Milton Friedman made in connection with receiving the Nobel Prize might be meaningful in this context. He is saying that the situation in Great Britain is ripe for a takeover from either extreme of the political spectrum. This will centralise the power in the State and bring about change for the survival of the system consistent with the values of the group forcing the change.

Another point that comes to mind is a psychological point associated

An Apology for Change

with encounter groups (Schutz 1976). It says that everyone is responsible for their own behaviour. Therefore, everyone, including a nation, is where they want to be. This is true even if that place appears as undesirable to them or to others. The logic behind this is that there is some comfort even in undesirable places: at least it is our own undesirableness; at least it is an undesirableness that I know the limits of and can compensate for. According to this theory, the resistance to change in British organisations is not due to American change technology being too American. Nor is it due to the value system of the British resisting change as defined in organisational development terms. Rather, according to this thinking, British organisations are where the British want them. It is important to the British that their organisations be as they are, and British organisations will stay the way they are until the British decide they want to change them. At that time, the British will also learn how to change them.

We must count as real that some cultural values, which have many positive attributes, are blocks to the organisational development type of change that seems to be the current technology for changing organisations. But that does not have to lead to the conclusion that change cannot take place through this technology. Other European countries have changed their work places (Harrison 1976). They have done it by experimenting, effecting new agreements between management and workers, and only recently putting workers on the board. There is a lot of hard work ahead in order to discover the most effective way to change organisations in the United Kingdom.

Unconscious collusion

In addition to the issues discussed so far, there is a more academic argument with far reaching implications. That argument is about the most effective method for implementing change in the behaviour of an organisation. Greiner (1967) states that much of the change literature praises the change programmes which use massive training programmes to bring about change. His own thesis is that change frequently occurs as a result of the antecedents of such programmes. He feels that the change can be traced to such conditions as historical aspects of the organisation or to the style and ability of management.

Ideas such as those of Greiner raise the issue of whether or not training individuals in new behaviour results in changed organisations. Katz and Kahn (1966) also doubt that training individuals in new behaviours results in changed organisations. They make a strong case that the most effective method of changing an organisation is to change the systemic variables of the organisation. By this they mean changing the actual way that an organisation conducts its work. For instance if humanising the work place is the change programme, and union/management relations are poor, begin with the planning as a joint effort of unions and management (see Ottaway 1976 for a detailed strategy for change of the systemic type). Establishing new training programmes is less difficult at the outset but more difficult to use to effect change in the behaviour of the organisation.

After reviewing seven different approaches to changing organisations, Katz and Kahn (1966, p. 449) conclude:

> The study and the accomplishment of organisational change has been handicapped by the tendency to disregard systemic properties of organisations and to confuse individual change with change in organisational variables. More specifically, scientists and practitioners have assumed too often that an individual change will produce a corresponding organisational change. This assumption seems to us indefensible.

To summarise the root of the unconscious collusion, it is that training has been highlighted by organisational change proponents as the most effective approach. Also, it is known that establishing training programmes is easier for the client system to accept as change and easier for the consultant to get the client to establish. This root problem is then exacerbated by the method that is commonly used by organisations to select consultants to assist them in changing.

The unconscious collusion becomes a reality at the point of contracting between the change agent (consultant) and the changee (client system). This process usually begins with a manager in the organisation being charged with 'finding the right person to help us'. Typically, the manager contacts several consultants and tells each of them that he and his organisation are committed to change of a far reaching nature. Negotiations are conducted over several meetings. In the early discussions the manager is trying to find out exactly how the consultant would go about the programme. At this time the consultant is trying to decide what it is the manager wants.

The credibility of the change agent is a central issue. The manager needs to be assured that the proposed programme will work. He is to be judged by his peers by that criteria. The consultant responds to this by suggesting a training programme as a readiness phase. This meets the manager's needs and will not upset the system too much. The consult-

An Apology for Change

ant knows that it will get him in and he hopes for real change later by the systemic approach after the client's system is more prepared for it by the training programme.

The manager will then invite proposals from several consultants who have passed the first test of being documented in the literature of the behavioural sciences and making a non-threatening suggested start-point. Sometimes these proposals are presented to a group of the manager's superiors and peers by a short list of consultants. The colluding aspect of this procedure is that the consultant is participating in a process which will only allow a minimal, individually oriented change programme to take place.

A training oriented consultant gets the contract and training takes place. It is found useful by many in their individual work. Many have been included in a nice perk: namely, going to a three-star hotel for a week of training. All in all, it shows up the consultant and the manager as effective and the organisation has a feeling of something good happening. Then a colleague in another firm rings up the manager to inquire about a good consultant to help them change the organisation to a more participative style work place. The manager suggests that his colleague talk to their consultant who is doing a good job. The cycle starts all over again.

One of the reasonable critiques that doubting managers make is that change programmes do not work. They say that sending all those managers off for training does not do one thing to reduce industrial disputes, labour turnover, production costs and so on. Organisation change and development practitioners have been guilty of too much training and not enough change. But the guilt is on both sides of the contract. Managers are too often afraid to take the first step required to bring about significant change. Training is a hope held by change agents and client systems that change can be easy. Who is going to be the first to break this collusion? Is management going to say we need change agents who are capable of helping us change our way of working together? Are OD consultants going to risk saying that a systemic change is required and not collude with management's fear by suggesting training programmes? Maybe the unions will see a role for themselves here and break the collusion.

Conclusions

At the end of this apology I feel that we have covered a lot of ground with one recurring theme: change is a frightening experience and we find a lot of reasons not to get involved in it. All the reasons we give for not changing are based on some truth. There are disappointing results from too many change programmes. The amenities of Great Britain are missing in more change oriented cultures. Americans do step forward with their way of work and managing as *the* way. Change for the sake of change does happen when some managers do not know what else to do. The technology we use for changing organisations is limited and underdeveloped for the task at hand.

But most of the reasoning about each truth is a myth. That is, the reasons given cover up the unmentionable truth that the British have not, for the most part, found it in their self-interest to change the work place as drastically as have other cultures. Most of the reasons given can also be seen as fears. Fears of change are based on lack of understanding it.

References

Coch, L. and French, J.R.P. Jr., 'Overcoming Resistance to Change', *Human Relations*, Vol. I, No. 4 (1948).
Harrison, R., *Worker Participation In Western Europe* (Institute of Personnel Management, London, 1976.)
Jones, G.N., *Planned Organisational Change* (Routledge and Kegan Paul, London, 1969.)
Kahn, R.L., 'Organisation Development. Some Problems and Proposals', *Journal of Applied Behavioural Science*, Vol. 10, No. 4 (1974).
Katz, D. and Kahn, R.L., *The Social Psychology of Organisations* (John Wiley and Sons, Inc., New York, 1966).
Morse, N. and Reimer, E., 'The Experimental Change of a Major Organisational Variable', *Journal of Abnormal and Social Psychology*, Vol. 52 (1956).
Ottaway, R.N., 'A Change Strategy to implement new norms', *Personnel Review*, Vol. 5, No. 1 (Winter, 1976).
Richardson, A., *Christian Apologetics* (S.C.M. Press Ltd., London, 1947).
Rogers, C.R., *The Application of Client-Centred Therapy* (Constable, London, 1961). *Freedom to Learn,* (Charles E. Merrill Publishing Co., Columbus, Ohio, 1969).
Schutz, W., *Elements of Encounter* Bantam Books, New York, 1975.
Spender, S., *Love-Hate Relations,* A Study of Anglo-American Sensibilities (Hammish Hamilton, London, 1974).
Steele, F., 'Is Organisation Development Work Possible In The U.K. Culture?', *Journal of European Training*, Vol. 5, No. 3 (1976).
Trist, E. and Bamforth, R., 'Some Social And Psychological Consequences of the Long Wall Method of Coal Cutting', *Human Relations*, Vol. 4, No. 1 (1951).

2 TECHNOLOGICAL DETERMINISM

John Langrish

There are various assumptions behind a book about 'humanising the work place'. One of these is that it is possible to make the work place different from the way that it is now.

The purpose of this chapter is to explore the nature of technological change, to consider whether technology really can be altered in a more 'human' direction or whether the nature of technology so controls the rest of society that the idea of free choice in selecting a different technology turns out to be illusory.

Many factors may stand in the way of humanising the work place including the social, political and economic systems which affect the nature of the work place. The point of view, known as technological determinism, considers that all these factors are themselves determined by the nature of technology so that any major change in the structure of society is impossible without a change in the technology.

Examples from the past have been used to support the idea of technological determinism. Thus Lynn White (1962) has attempted to demonstrate that the entire feudal system was the result of one technological change viz. the stirrup. (The stirrup made cavalry a superior fighting unit to Roman style foot soldiers. This meant that a society wishing to survive needed horses. Horses have to be fed in winter. This needs land which was parcelled out in return for military service with the horse soldier knight becoming a key figure in society.)

White makes the even more startling claim that the Renaissance was due to a technological change in the method of food production, increasing the protein content of European diet and giving people enough mental energy to be creative in addition to just surviving. In White's words, Europe at the time of the Renaissance was 'full of beans'.

Less spectacular claims for technological determinism are such ideas as the destruction of the feudal system by gunpowder and the cannon, railways causing the modern city, the steam engine and coal leading to a factory based society and so on.

These ideas represent a very simple form of technological determinism in which inventions or groups of inventions result directly in massive changes in social, political and economic systems. This simple technological determinism may be countered by a variety of arguments:

Where do the inventions come from? The use of inventions is determined by other systems — the Chinese did not use their gunpowder. Or today we can say that inventions now come from science so we can choose what inventions we want.

A more sophisticated view of technological determinism which is much harder to refute is Technological Darwinism. According to this view, inventions occur in large numbers by a random process analogous to gene mutation in biological evolution. Most inventions are never used. Those that are used survive because they impart some survival value to the users. Eventually, everyone who is in competition with the users of the new technology has to follow suit or cease to survive. If using the new technology means changing social, political or economic systems there is no choice, the new technology and all its consequences are adopted or extinction follows.

Thus the English cottage weavers had no choice when the factory-based textile industry emerged; they either starved or went to work in the factory. Even if they could have burned down the factories, this would only have delayed things until some other factory-based system overcame them either through the strength of a factory-based army or through the commercial strength of cheaper goods.

It is not fashionable these days to pay serious attention to this concept of technological determinism but any discussion of humanising the work place has to answer the question, just how free is man to alter his technology? David Dickson (1974) dismisses technological determinism. He has two main arguments against it which may be described as 'the Greeks knew about steam' argument and the Marxist view.

Such facts as the ancient Greeks knowing about steam engines, or the Chinese knowing about gunpowder, are quoted to show that inventions by themselves do not necessarily lead to the use of inventions and that some other factor determines whether the invention is used or not. This other factor then becomes the determinant of technology and technological determinism can be forgotten about. In the theory of technological Darwinism, however, most inventions are never used; those that are used become developed because they convey some advantage to the users. Labour saving inventions, for example, convey little advantage in societies with a plentiful supply of slaves or other cheap labour. In the same way that white bears had to wait the arrival of climatic changes before being white was an advantage, so many inventions have remained unused until a set of conditions gave them some survival value or advantage.

The conditions that decide whether a particular invention has an

Technological Determinism

advantage are complex and varied, including not just economic factors but also strategic, political and social factors. Within this complex advantage system, it is possible for technology to evolve in a manner which leaves little room for free will within the process.

One of the competitive advantages of a large-scale factory system is that it enables products to be exported. If 'humanising' the factory enables more cars to be exported then 'humanising' will happen. If 'humanising' actually results in fewer exports, it won't happen unless it has some other advantage. The fact that some people want it to happen is not a sufficient condition for such a change to take place and to that extent man is gripped by the force of technological determinism. The only other alternatives are to cease car manufacture or to isolate our society from competition with others.

Dickson's second objection to technological determinism takes the conventional Marxist approach which is to stress the economic causes of technological change. Although Marx was very much aware of how the nature of technology (means of production) can have a profound effect on the structure of society (relations of production) Dickson claims that Marx was not a technological determinist. Marx 'repeatedly stresses that it is not technology which makes it necessary for the capitalist to accumulate, but the need for accumulation which makes him develop the powers of technology'.

One of the problems of saying that the need for something led to a technical change is that the need corresponds to the advantage. Any surviving technology must have some advantage. After the event, that advantage can be interpreted as a need which was present before the technology and which led to the development of the technology. This is a classic Adam's navel or chicken and egg dichotomy. Does the need for the advantage produce the technology or does the technology produce the advantage and hence the awareness of a need for that advantage?

Fortunately (for the purposes of this discussion that is) Dickson's objection to technological determinism can be refuted without getting involved in chicken and egg arguments. Quite simply, Dickson does not appreciate the nature of Technological Darwinism which does not claim that new technology made it necessary for the capitalist to accumulate.

Technological Darwinism, which Dickson does not refute, regards the early beginnings of both the factory system and the capitalist system as arriving by quite independent mechanisms. Once the two systems coincided, the survival value of factory technology became apparent. Other societies, in order to survive, found that they must have factories. In order to get factories they found they needed capital accumulation as well, in order to gather the resources necessary for the technology.

Once this happened, societies in competition with others ceased to have freedom of choice. In order to compete, they needed the technology with survival value and as long as this technology requires capital accumulation for its functioning, they have to be that sort of society. This is not the same as saying that technology made the capitalist accumulate in the first place, but once the two have come together, the effect is the same, the nature of society can not easily be changed; it is 'determined' by the technology. Associated with the rise of factories is the development of the division of labour which made factory-based technologies more competitive. Again, societies in competition had no alternative, they were forced to adopt the division of labour and its consequences.

A good illustration of the way that the nature of a society is more in the grip of its technology of production than any other factor is provided by the way in which the societies of USA and USSR are moving closer together in certain important aspects.

In order to compete successfully, both societies have found it necessary to move away from their original conceptions towards a direction in which they become more like each other.

This 'convergence' view of American and Russian societies has been expressed by several writers. W.S. Buckingham (1958), from the point of view of economics, concluded that the two economic systems were growing more similar. P.A. Sorokin (1964), the American sociologist, has concluded that future society and culture are likely to be neither capitalist nor communist but a new type, intermediary between the two existing forms.

Galbraith's (1967) view of industrial society is well known. He considers that the demands made by technology are more important than the concepts of capitalism and socialism. He has described how decision-making in both systems is becoming a similar process, with more decentralisation in Russia and more centralisation in the States producing the 'technostructure' required to maintain modern technological society.

If societies as apparently dissimilar as those of Russia and America (not to mention many others throughout the world) are evolving in a similar direction, it seems reasonable to look for a common factor. There is such a factor, namely their technology, which is capital intensive and based on the division of labour. Galbraith claims that 'nearly all of the consequences of modern technology ... derive from this need to divide and subdivide tasks.'

A discussion of technological determinism is therefore crucial to any discussion of humanising the work place. If the work place is in need of humanising because it has been dehumanised through the division of labour, the central question becomes why did this process of dehumanisation take place? The technological determinist answer is that societies in competition had no choice; division of labour and dehumanisation were required for a more competitive technology. Alternative answers are that dehumanisation was caused by capitalist society or that it happened because no one bothered to stop it, i.e. that no one was very worried about it until recently.

The latter alternative is just not true. Even Adam Smith predicted that the division of labour would make life more boring for the workers. Marx wrote about the alienation of the workers and the following quotation from the Shop Stewards Movement of 1919 shows that at least some workers have been resisting dehumanisation for a long time:

> Under the guise of scientific management, the Capitalists are introducing into industry schemes for dividing operations, and making labour more automatic. The result of this tendency is to deny the worker responsibility, rob him of initiative and reduce him to the level of some ghastly, inhuman, mechanical puppet. (Quoted by Elliot and Elliot, 1976, p. 33.)

Thus as long ago as 1919, workers were objecting to 'inhuman' practices and blaming them on 'the Capitalists'. However, the 'nasty Capitalist' hypothesis is not a good one. Lenin made a study of the 'scientific management' techniques of F.W. Taylor which were based on work-study and the sub-division of manual tasks. Lenin's conclusion in 1918 was that, 'We must organise in Russia the study and teaching of the Taylor system.' Being in a state of competition with the rest of the world, Russia had to use the most efficient form of technology available to it; if this meant dehumanising the work place, there was not much choice.

Technological determinism, therefore, suggests that the work place can not be humanised without a drastic change in technology and that this change will not take place unless some new form of technology appears with a greater survival value than existing forms. Just the desire to change technology is not sufficient: technology is not so easily controlled. Nor will changing society either, through revolution or gradual change, lead to a humanised work place unless the technology is changed first.

How could such a technological change take place? There are two ways. First, the dehumanising aspects of modern technology may proceed to the stage where the technology becomes less efficient than a new form of technology. Second, there is the possibility that a new form of technology will emerge through the random processes of technological evolution. If this form of technology survives because of some advantage not directly linked to the effect of technology on the worker, then a secondary side effect, almost by chance, might be the possibility of humanising the work place. The key to humanising the work place therefore becomes technological change, either change consciously directed at making the work place more human because it is believed that this will also be more efficient or change for some other reason which by chance produces a humanising influence.

It is necessary, therefore, to discuss what is known about the process of technological change.

The nature of technological change

If it could be shown that — like getting a man on the moon — society can now achieve any technological goal if it allocates enough resources to that end, then the case for technological determinism would be dead. Humanising the work place would then become a matter of gaining control of the resource allocation process to ensure that a 'human' technology is developed. The debate then becomes a matter of discussing rival forms of control of technology, worker directors versus total revolution, etc.

However, if technology really controls the political forms of society as suggested by technological determinism, then altering the political system will not of itself alter the technology.

What is the evidence? At first sight, recent studies of technological change seem to suggest that innovation is governed by 'need pull', i.e. if someone wants something strongly enough and has the necessary power they seem to get it. As this apparent conclusion is in direct conflict with technological determinism, it is necessary to mention these recent studies and show how the 'need pull' conclusion has been misunderstood.

As soon as the literature on technological innovation is examined, the chicken and egg discussion reappears on the scene. Many forms of this discussion exist but the central theme is the question of whether changes in technology come about as a result of some independent

Technological Determinism

process — science, invention, creativity and the like, or whether change takes place because someone wants it to happen and is in a position to allocate resources to make sure that it does happen.

Although it is fairly obvious that both of these conditions need to exist, there has been much discussion about which comes first or which determines the other. There are, in effect, two rival views of the process whereby new forms of technology arrive and become established.

Supporters of what might be called a 'discovery push' view of innovation see technological change as consisting of a series of steps such as pure science, applied science, invention, development, manufacture, marketing, distribution and profit.

The rival view, need pull, as expressed by Holloman (1965) states:

> The sequence — perceived need, invention, innovation (limited by political, social or economic forces) and diffusion or adaptation (determined by the organisational character and incentives of industry) — is the one most often met in the regular civilian economy.

Utterback (1974) has examined eight studies of technological innovation, each of which was based on several innovations. He categorises the conclusions of these studies as seeing innovation as being produced by either need or technical opportunity (discovery push) and produces the following table.

Study	Proportion of innovations from market, mission or production needs %	Proportion from technical opportunities %
Baker et al.	77	23
Carter & Williams	73	27
Goldhar	69	31
Sherwin & Isenson	66	34
Langrish et al.	66	34
Myers & Marquis	78	22
Tannenbaum et al.	90	10
Utterback	75	25

Thus widely differing studies, covering different countries, different industries and different degrees of change apparently agree that need pull is more important than discovery push. If this were true, innovation should be a controllable process — identify the need, acquire the resources and produce the new technology.

Economists have also discussed technical change in terms of two rival theories, innovation as resulting from factors outside the economic system versus innovation 'pulled' by economic demand. The strongest supporter of the latter view has been Schmookler (1966).

This debate in economics has been expressed by Rosenburg (1976) in terms used in other contexts viz. supply and demand. Rosenburg interprets Schmookler as claiming that the rate of production of inventions is governed by demand. He challenges the conclusion that might be inferred from Schmookler by drawing attention to the restrictions on the supply of really new things from science.

In effect, Rosenburg claims that there has always been a demand for better health, more efficient manufacture, cheaper energy etc. This demand does not govern the supply of innovations until the time is right and this time is determined by non-economic factors.

Other forms of this push-pull debate have centred round the planning of R & D by Governments and Companies. In the 1960s, there was a huge increase in expenditure, both public and private, on scientific research. Apparently, it was believed that putting more resources into science started off a process that ultimately resulted in economic growth. However, this view has not been justified and it is much more difficult for scientists to get away with the dogmatic assertions that they used to make about the impossibility of planning science. Both private industry and Government are now more reluctant to spend money on research that does not fit some stated need.

Thus it might seem that need pull has won the day over discovery push. However, a more detailed look at the process of technological change reveals that much of the push-pull debate is rather sterile, resulting from over simplification of the complex processes involved. Attempts to force real life situations into one of two simple linear models distinguished by different starting points are not very useful for the following three reasons.

1. The multiplicity of needs and pushes

In the real world there is no simple market place where needs for new ideas and producers of new ideas get together. There are perceived needs, imaginary needs, latent needs and manipulated needs. Also different groups have different needs which may be in conflict.

Similarly, there is no single mechanism supplying the new ideas. The tendency to use 'science and technology' as though it were one word, hides the fact that there are separate processes with different aims operating within this label.

One of the studies (Langrish *et al.* 1972) mentioned by Utterback in his review, looked at UK organisations which had received the Queen's Award to Industry for Technological Innovation. This study attempted to distinguish between two types of discovery push — from science or technology and two types of need pull — needs of the customer and needs of the innovator, but the important conclusion of this attempt which is not mentioned by Utterback, is that of the 84 innovations studied, very few fitted unambiguously into any of these models, a point that leads to the second objection.

2. Innovation is not a simple linear process

In addition to the mixture of pushes and pulls that seem to affect the process of innovation in general, the complex pathways leading to a specific change in technology also contain a variety of events. Some characterisable as pushes from invention, discovery or the like and some characterisable as pulls from such directions as the strategic needs of a country, the needs of a customer, the needs of an individual in a position to allocate resources and so on. It is only by arbitrarily selecting one event as The Start of the process that it is possible to categorise an innovation as the result of a single linear process of a particular kind.

The 'Wealth from Knowledge' study showed that the kind of innovations that gained the Queen's Award to Industry were usually based on at least three important technical concepts rather than a single 'invention' or 'discovery'. The origins of these concepts lay in different places at different times and occurred in response to different sorts of stimuli. Under such circumstances, the description of a specific technological innovation as being in response to a single demand or the result of a single creative act is a gross over-simplification.

An example will illustrate the complex mixture of processes which lead to a change in technology. Consider the hypodermic syringe, as used in hospitals. At one time, they were made of glass and sterilised by heat treatment between successive uses. Today they are mainly made of plastic, supplied to the hospital in a sterile condition and thrown away after one use. A change has taken place but how did it happen?

At first glance, throw away hypodermics may seem to be just an extension of the throw away plastic concept made possible by the availability of new materials, processing machinery and customers capable of buying things in large numbers and throwing them away. It is true that the pioneer of the disposable hypodermic, Roy Glasson, was working in the plastics processing industry but before he could produce a satisfactory product he had to solve problems not usually met with in disposable plastics.

Glasson's two major problems were the metal needles and the method of sterilisation. The problem of a supply of very cheap disposable needles was met by a Japanese company. Various methods of sterilisation were possible but Glasson finally settled for the use of cobalt-60 irradiation, pioneered by the Canadians but developed by the UK Atomic Energy Authority. The commercial use of cobalt-60 sterilisation was made possible by a small family firm, H.S. Marsh, with the expertise in mechanical handling necessary for moving packages of hypodermics round the cobalt-60 radiation source in an efficient manner.

Thus there was no single invention or discovery of a useful disposable hypodermic syringe. This complexity has been recognised by several writers. A.P. Usher (1955), for example, discussing the varied inputs to the process, claimed 'the vocabulary of common speech does not supply convenient words to express an achievement spread over time in a number of steps. The best we can do is to use the plural form "secondary inventions".'

Usher's secondary inventions are those which extend the use of an underlying primary invention. However, in practice, such a distinction turns out to be not too helpful. In the case of the disposable syringe, what is the primary invention? It partly depends on the point of view of the observer. The disposable syringe can be seen as a secondary invention extending the replacement of glass by plastics; it can also be seen as a secondary invention extending the use of radioactive isotopes. From the point of view of the Japanese firm supplying the needles, it is extending the use of a development in metal forming.

The situation is still more complex than a mixture of viewpoints. Even from one specific viewpoint, there is no clearly definable primary invention. The use of radio isotopoes has complex origins. Sterilisation by irradiation predates knowledge of isotopes; sunlight, ultra-violet radiation and X-rays had all been found to have germ-killing properties before gamma radiation from radioactive isotopes was investigated.

Similarly, the replacement of glass by plastics has no single primary invention; there are a variety of plastic materials and a variety of ways of processing them, each with a complex history (the moulding of thermoplastics dates back at least as far as the use of metal signet rings to form and cool molten wax).

The above account illustrates the complexity of the invention push

Technological Determinism

process. A similar complexity exists on the need pull side. The UKAEA had an organisational need to find commercial uses for radio isotopes. Glasson had a personal need to diversify, H.S. Marsh, a family firm, had an organisational need to diversify coupled with a personal interest in solving interesting technical problems. Commercial success was assisted by the existence of the National Health Service with centralised purchasing of hospital supplies.

Thus the single technological change represented by the plastic hypodermic syringe is itself a coming together of many other changes both social and technological. To place such an example in a box marked 'demand determines supply' or 'discovery pushes use' says more about the person selecting the box than it does about the nature of innovation.

3. Innovations vary in degree of change

We have discussed two reasons for discounting the Utterback conclusion that need determines technological change in opposition to the concept of technological determinism.

A third reason for being wary about this conclusion is the possibility that the process which results in a small number of large changes is different from the process which produces the large numbers of small changes. In terms of the effect of technology on society, a small number of innovations, electric power, synthetic materials, the assembly line, antibiotics etc. have produced great impacts. The vast number of innovations, however, seem to have little impact on their own.

The sort of studies listed by Utterback are concerned mainly with 'small change' innovations but the Queen's Award study did suggest that the small number of 'large change' innovations included in its sample, were much more describable in terms of discovery push than were the majority 'small change' innovations.

One study which has been aimed at these large change innovations is Mensch (1971). He has shown that large change innovations appear in cycles separated by periods of little change. The last period of intense change was 1935-45; in those ten years, there were more large innovations than in the thirty years since. Television, the jet engine, antibiotics, a new generation of synthetic materials, radar and atomic energy are amongst the innovations that belong to that period. No comparable list can be drawn up for the thirty years since then. Mensch also describes earlier periods of intense change and it might be that we are about to see the start of another such period.

Now, the degree of technical change that took place during 1935-45 is most easily explained by reference to the war, including preparation for it. But there is perhaps a more fundamental explanation which is to say that there was a change in the advantage system which determines whether an invention has any survival value.

Thus, although ways of manufacturing synthetic rubber-like materials as an alternative to collecting natural rubber from trees had been known for several years, it was not until the Japanese captured the rubber plantations that synthetic rubber had much in the way of an advantage. The availability of a cheap and plentiful supply of plantation rubber had held back developments in synthetic rubber but the loss of the plantations led to the rapid development of synthetic rubbers in the States and Canada, using government money. It was only in Germany and Russia that any appreciable quantities of synthetic rubber were manufactured before the 1939-45 war. In both these countries there was a strategic advantage to the government in moving away from dependence on foreign controlled supplies of natural rubber. In Soviet Russia, the government controlled industry so it was fairly simple to ignore the extra cost of synthetic rubber. In Nazi Germany, with a theoretically independent industry, the government was able to manipulate the advantage system by imposing an import duty on natural rubber to make it more expensive than synthetic.

The appearance of a new industry, manufacturing synthetic rubbers on a large scale, took place between 1935-45 not because of new discoveries (the sodium-catalysed polymerisation of butadiene to give 'Buna' rubber was known in England and Germany prior to 1914 and prior to the scientific concept of polymerisation) but because of changes in the advantage system that took place during that time.

Following the war, it might have been thought that the advantage or survival value of synthetic rubber would have disappeared. However, the availability of raw materials from the new oil-based petrochemical industry together with economies of scale from large capacity plants established during the war meant that synthetic rubber could continue to compete with natural rubber even when the plantations were re-established.

Most of the major innovations that appeared between 1935 and 1945 made use of government money in one form or another. In the years since the war, government expenditure on R & D has increased several fold so the reason for the much smaller number of major innovations is not that governments lost interest in technical change once the war was over.

The major innovation peak of 1935-45 and three earlier peaks detected by Mensch are not explicable in terms of peaks of inventive activity or creativity. Mensch demonstrates this by listing the dates of the inventions on which he sees his innovations as being based. The distribution over time of the basic inventions shows no peaks.

The attempt to view a major innovation (like the manufacture of synthetic rubber) as being based on one invention at one point in time (like Buna rubber's laboratory preparation in 1912) is a particularly hazardous occupation because of the complexity of innovation and the multiplicity of technical inputs. Nonetheless the absence of peaks in Mensch's data for his inventions suggests that we must look elsewhere for an explanation of peaks of innovation.

The viewpoint of Technological Darwinism can be used to explain Mensch's findings. If inventions occur randomly in large numbers and only a small number survive, the timing of important inventions should depend on the survival conditions and not the invention-producing mechanism. In a period of sudden climatic change, various animal variations that already exist will become important for survival. The 1935-45 period corresponds to a climatic change in that the rules of survival or the conditions of the advantage system were subject to massive change. Under these circumstances, technical ideas which already existed in many cases, acquired some advantage over other technical ideas and were hence made of use.

Since about 1950, until recently the technical climate has remained comparatively stable, held by two forces, the availability of low cost oil and the advantages of larger scale units of production. Under these circumstances, major technological innovation has been unlikely; it has been very difficult for a new technology to find an advantage over existing technology. The hovercraft, for example, is a radically new method of transport and its development has been assisted by government money. Novelty, however, is not enough; several firms have now lost money through trying to find competitive advantages from the hovercraft. Dashing around a few inches into the air may be fun but the cost of doing this is not really justified by any major advantage over less novel ways of moving about.

Technological paradigms

If the Mensch cycles continue to repeat themselves, we could be about to experience another period in which major innovation again becomes possible. An analogy can be drawn between periods of large technical change interspersed with periods of improvements within an existing framework and Thomas Kuhn's (1970) view of the evolution of science which he describes as having periods of revolution interspersed with periods of 'normal' science. Normal science, in Kuhn's view, consists of a period in which the basic concepts or paradigms of science are agreed, used and slightly modified. In a period of revolutionary science, the paradigms cease to work and have to be replaced by new ones.

The nineteenth century factory system of technology can be seen as an example of a technological paradigm. The advantages of power-driven machines situated in factories were such that considerable technological change took place to enable factory systems to be established in most industries. Once this had occurred, the amount of radical change became less. The efficiency of the new methods of manufacture was such that it was difficult, if not impossible, to compete with them using older manufacturing methods. Also, it was difficult to find competitive new alternative methods of manufacture. A stable paradigm had been established not to be changed even by revolution.

The last twenty-five years of technological history can be seen as a stable period governed by the paradigm of economies of scale which itself has rested on assumptions about continuing growth and cheap supplies of energy. An important point which this chapter seeks to demonstrate is that in such a stable period major technological change, whether in a more human direction or in any other direction, is not possible. Such change has to wait until the governing paradigm ceases to work; this may be about to happen with the drive for economies of scale.

The basic concept of economies of scale is that if one manufactures a thousand articles or a thousand tons of something per year in a plant of that capacity, the manufacturing cost per article or per ton is less than if one has a plant which only produces one hundred per year. Ten plants capable of manufacturing a hundred cost more to build and to run than one capable of manufacturing a thousand.

There are two main reasons why economies of scale can be obtained. The first is a geometric concept that doubling the scale of something increases the surface area by four times, but increases the volume by eight times. If the cost depends on the surface area but the capacity on the volume then economies of scale are obtained i.e. it is cheaper to provide one container or reaction vessel for a thousand gallons than it is to provide ten one hundred gallon containers. Similarly it is cheaper to heat one large factory, oven, reaction vessel or office than several smaller separate ones because the heat escapes from the surface. (Imagine eight cubic ovens all losing heat from their surfaces. If the eight cubes are put together to make a larger 2x2x2 cube, the amount of surface and hence

Technological Determinism

the amount of heat loss is diminished.)

The second cause of economies of scale is the sharing of fixed costs amongst a larger number. If it costs a million pounds to make the moulds in which steel is pressed to form a car body and if only one car body is made from these moulds, the addition to the cost of the car is a million pounds. However if a million car bodies are made from the moulds then the additional cost is only one pound per car.

Economies of scale need not be expressed in terms of money. Even a society which had found an alternative to money would have to consider the allocation of resources and one large scale piece of technology may use less energy or less material for construction than several smaller ones.

It follows that where competition exists, increasing the scale of technology has provided survival value or advantage over smaller scale production. Much technological change in the last twenty-five years has been directed towards increasing the scale of units of production rather than to finding radically new ways of doing things. If this increase in scale has been accompanied by more dehumanisation, there has been little choice; the more human smaller scale operations have become like species of animals in danger of extinction, i.e. only surviving when protected from competition. Similarly, where such an increase in scale has been accompanied by the removal of dangerous and unpleasant working conditions, this has been a fortuitous benefit and not the result of people wanting such changes.

Under such circumstances, major technological change now seems apparently impossible. A really new synthetic fibre, for example, has little chance of getting into production. Manufacture would have to start on a fairly small scale and this would make the new fibre very much more expensive than existing fibres which are manufactured on a massive scale.

A really new type of motor car, produced by a really new method (not just the minor change represented by the Volvo experiment) would have to start with small scale production and would not be able to compete with the existing large scale manufacturing, distribution and maintenance systems.

One way of overcoming this problem of introducing new technology is the use of Government finance in the early stages until the scale of operations can reach the size where it is competitive. Thus synthetic rubber in its early years was very much more expensive than natural rubber. Government action in Russia, Germany and the States was required to enable the scale of synthetic rubber manufacture to reach such a size that it could compete.

In this country we have the NRDC (National Research & Development Council) to provide Government finance for the early stages of new technological developments. However, the NRDC has not been able to find a vast number of new ideas worth developing. It has been very difficult to find new ways of doing things that offer some advantage over established ways of doing things. The hovercraft, for example, which has received substantial support from NRDC is not really a better form of transport than existing methods. Four firms have gone bankrupt in attempting to develop the hovercraft (Johnson, 1974).

It would seem, therefore, that in the present period of technology, even Government finance is not enough to ensure the survival of really new technologies. New technologies have to wait until something disturbs the stability of the existing systems.

The basic question for those interested in humanising the work place becomes a matter of asking what are the chances of something reducing the advantages of the present system to such an extent that new experimental ways of doing things have a chance of survival?

There are now many signs that the advantages of the present systems of technology are breaking down. The major problem with the drive for economies of scale is matching output to capacity. The larger the capacity of the plant, the less likely it is that the desired output will actually be the same as the capacity.

In a growing market, it is possible to construct a plant with a capacity greater than that of the market demand and wait for demand to increase. It is also possible to stimulate demand with consequent effects on the nature of a society being forced to consume more in order to ensure the advantage of its ruling form of technology.

However, if several competitors attempt to do this, there is a massive over capacity in the industry and competition forces price cutting until the growth in the market absorbs the spare capacity at which point, if growth continues, there is substantial under capacity. The drive for economies of scale then forces several competitors to build even larger plants, hoping to gain reduced production costs and undercut their competitors to gain an increased share of the growing market. The resultant over capacity is then greater than the original; an economist's equilibrium point is nowhere in sight.

The polymer producing industry is an example of an industry which has lurched from over capacity to under capacity. In the process, several firms have withdrawn from the industry but those who remain have not found the industry to be very profitable.

When an increasing price of oil is added to the system together with

Technological Determinism

political uncertainty about the future of oil producing countries and the probability of these countries financing their own production facilities, then the huge petrochemical complex, of which polymer production forms a part, looks extremely unstable.

New ways of making the raw materials for polymer production will eventually emerge as oil becomes more scarce and more expensive. Such new ways as may emerge could well be much smaller in scale and capable of greater variety. They might also be adaptable to a zero growth economy. If this happened, certain jobs would become more enjoyable. The research worker could again attempt to find new polymers and new ways of making polymers with some chance of his work being used. The manager of a new, small entrepreneurial organisation would make meaningful decisions instead of being a part of an international giant.

For such people, the work place could be said to have become more human but if this happened it would not be because people are wanting the work place to become more human but because the dominant form of technology produced such a result as a side effect.

There are other signs that the forms of technology possessing survival value are moving in the direction of a smaller scale of production. A special case occurs in industries with little growth in total market. Two such industries in this country are bread and beer production. In such industries, the drive for economies of scale in production has taken the form of takeovers and amalgamations resulting in the replacement of small independent bakeries and breweries by large ones. Economies of scale in production have been obtained and at one time it seemed as though small scale production could only survive as an expensive luxury for speciality products.

However, there are now signs that this trend is being reversed. The reduction in unit manufacturing costs obtained by concentrating production at fewer sites is being countered by an increase in other unit costs, particularly transport. (If say eight small factories in eight small towns are replaced by one central factory, eight times as large as the small ones, then unit production costs can be decreased. However, the output from the new large factory has to be transported to the eight small towns, causing an increase in transport costs.)

Transport costs have become increasingly important in recent years, mainly as a result of increased petrol prices but also because centralised distribution systems have made trade union activity more possible and more costly. The brewing industry in particular has been hit by several strikes amongst distribution workers.

Instead of the products of local breweries becoming too expensive for survival, the reverse is now possible. In Manchester, for example, the independent local brewery sells its products at a lower price than the nationally advertised brands; this low price being mainly the result of lower unit transport costs in a small but concentrated distribution system.

The large breweries are also suffering from consumer resistance to the products of their technology. In order to gain economies of scale, the technologies involved in brewing, storage and distribution have changed. These changes have not only altered the process technologies, they have led to changes in the product which are now being resisted by such pressures as the Campaign for Real Ale (CAMRA).

An interesting development in the baking industry is the growth of new small scale baking equipment used at retail outlets to bake a day's supply, hence cutting out the cost of daily transport from a central bakery. It could be that being a baker in charge of one's own shop and responsible for one's own production is a more human occupation than being part of a crowd working at a large bakery. (Alternatively, of course, it might be regarded as a more stressful, lonely and hazardous occupation.)

Another major reason for suggesting that smaller forms of technology may be acquiring some advantage is the lack of flexibility of large scale technology. In a stable period, it is possible to invest large sums in huge plants believing that current trends will continue to justify the investment. However, in a period of uncertainty, such as the present, there may be major changes in the costs and availability of raw materials, energy supplies and markets. When such changes occur, as they last did around 1940, there is a major survival value in flexibility, but highly specialised technologies designed to achieve economies of scale through the production of large numbers of one product do not possess such flexibility. Survival will pass to those smaller, less specialised, forms of technology able to adapt, or to alternative technologies already invented but currently possessing no advantage.

The concept of a technological paradigm may be linked to technological determinism. During the stable period of a successful paradigm, man has little choice e.g. 'small is beautiful' may have been desirable in the past but not possible until the 'large is cheap' paradigm begins to break down.

During such a period of stability, the small changes in technology that do take place may well approximate to a need pull view as long as the need and the change are not in conflict with the underlying paradigm.

However, a major change such as is represented by a form of technology that allows for humanising the work place has to wait the failure of the advantage of the current paradigm. The near future may witness this happening. If it does, for a brief period choice may be possible because once a new form of technology is required, different alternatives may be available, until one is selected and acquires a specific advantage over other alternatives, namely the advantage of being used.

It follows, therefore, that despite the claims for technological determinism expressed in this chapter, those interested in humanising the work place should act to ensure that a humanising choice is made. There may not be another opportunity for a very long time.

References

Buckingham, W.S., *Theoretical Economic Systems* (New York, 1958).
Dickson, D., *Alternative Technology* (Fontana, Glasgow, 1974).
Elliott, D. & Elliott, R., *The Control of Technology* (Wykeham Publications, London, 1976).
Galbraith, J.K., *The New Industrial State* (Boston, 1967).
Holloman, J.H. in R.A. Tybout (ed.), *Economics of Research & Development* (Ohio State U.P. Columbus, 1965).
Johnson, P.S., 'The Development of Hovercraft', *Three Banks Review*, Dec. 1974.
Kuhn, T.S., *The Structure of Scientific Revolutions* (University of Chicago Press, 2nd ed., 1970).
Langrish, J., Gibbons, M., Evans, W.G. & Jevons, F.R., *Wealth from Knowledge, A Study of Innovation in Industry* (Macmillan, London, 1972).
Lenin, V.I., *Collected Works* Vol. 20 p. 153 (Moscow, 1964).
Mensch, G., 'Zur Dynamik des technischen Fortschritts', *Betriebswirtschaft, 41*, p. 295 (1971).
Rosenburg, N., *Perspectives on Technology* (Cambridge U.P., 1976).
Schmookler, J., *Invention & Economic Growth* (Harvard U.P., 1966).
Sorokin, P.A., *The Basic Trends of Our Times* (Yale U.P., 1964).
Usher, A.P., *Capital Formation and Economic Growth* (National Bureau of Economic Research, 1955).
Utterback, C., 'Innovation in Industry and the Diffusion of Technology', *Science, 183* p. 620 (1974).
White, L., *Medieval Technology and Social Change* (Oxford U.P., 1962).

3 ARE COMPUTER SYSTEMS AND HUMANISED WORK COMPATIBLE?

Mary Weir

The popular view of computer-based systems is that of monolithic, unbelievably clever machines, which can also sometimes be incredibly stupid. When human beings are fitted into the picture, it is usually either as helpless slaves to the machines or as hapless victims of its silly mistakes. The basis of these views may be rather exaggerated, but nevertheless it contains an element of truth.

However, the reality of the development of computer-based systems over the last decade can hardly be exaggerated. From the limited, unsophisticated batch systems of early years, computer technology has developed rapidly and now provides dramatically improved possibilities for the collection, storage and processing of information for decision-making. Many batch systems are being enhanced to provide on-line access directly to the computer to speed the collection and distribution of data, while on-line systems provide remote terminals with updated information within seconds, and time-sharing enables hundreds of remote users to have simultaneous access to the processing power of the computer.

The impact of computer systems

The impact of such computer systems on work roles and organisation structures has been equally dramatic and far-reaching. Of course, there are considerable variations in the nature and degree of this impact depending on such factors as

— the structure of the organisation
— the type of work tasks being performed
— the needs, values and interests of the people employed
— the design of the system
— the strategy of implementation.

It might be helpful initially to explore the effects of existing computer-based systems on work organisation, before considering the opportunities which are available to use the potential of computer technology to improve the quality of working life.

Characteristics of modern organisations

Until recently, computer systems have been mainly introduced in large, modern organisations, which tend to have hierarchical and bureaucratic structures. Traditionally (Weber 1947) the characteristics of such organisations are to be seen in

- the hierarchical ranking of jobs and people
- the specialisation and fragmentation of work and functions
- the system of rules and procedures for all contingencies
- a high degree of impersonality in human relations.

The problems of bureaucratic organisations have been well documented (e.g. Gouldner 1954; Burns and Stalker 1961; Crozier 1964). The major problem, of course, is the extent to which such structures are rigid and inflexible, especially when faced with the need to introduce changes and cope with dynamic situations. Similarly, bureaucratic organisations are frequently subject to failures of information and communication, resulting from the degree of specialisation and the separation of functions, which make the transfer and feedback of information difficult. The specialisation and interdependence of tasks can often lead to inefficiency, in adhering to boundaries and goals which do not allow for the unpredictable events which are bound to occur. Perhaps most significant of all for the people employed in the organisation, bureaucratic structures do not provide conditions for individual motivation and self-development, since tasks and relationships are carefully prescribed and impersonal.

Such problems are so widespread in organisations that it is important to examine them in relation to the computer systems which many of them now operate.

Structural changes for computer systems

Many computer-based information systems have been designed and implemented in such a way that they have tended to emphasise the characteristics and problems of modern organisations. For example, Whisler (1970) has suggested that the introduction of computer systems has tended to result in the underlying structures and values of the organisation becoming more pronounced and powerful. In particular, where a major system is being introduced there may be significant structural changes in the organisation along traditional bureaucratic lines, and which then become fixed by the rigidity of the computer system. Such changes are usually a response to the need to organise the workflow for preparing input data for the computer and dealing with the output queries. Three main types of structural changes are readily visible

- the changes from 'parallel' to 'functional' departments
- the amalgamation and integration of departments
- a reduction in the number of hierarchical levels.

For example, there has been a restructuring of organisations from 'parallel' departments to 'functional' departments, which complements the bureaucratic principle of specialisation by function. Previously, departments were often structured so that they dealt with all or most of the functions related to a particular product or geographical area, with several departments in parallel to overcome problems of information and overload. However, the logic of computer technology and the greatly reduced cost of processing information has now created the tendency to move to a functional arrangement of departments, such as data control, data preparation, output handling and query departments.

For the people involved in these departments, however, this may very well be a change for the worse, since it is usually far more interesting to deal with a range of functions, while retaining close contact with particular customers or products, than to specialise on a functional area and tend to lose touch with the more personalised details. By fragmenting work in this way, the changes made to facilitate computer processing strengthen the traditional bureaucratic structure of the organisation. In addition, the tendency to deal for example with account numbers rather than names means that some of the interest is taken away from the job and the impersonality of the system is highlighted.

It is also quite common for several departments to be amalgamated, when their work is incorporated into an integrated computer information system. For example, a system may deal with several aspects of work such as order processing, customer accounting and stock reordering, and link them into an overarching system. The effect of integrating the work in this way is often to create such a close link between several departments, that they are amalgamated, especially when a reduction in staff is made. Inevitably such a change is accompanied by power struggles between the departments, as each tries to retain its autonomy and preserve its knowledge and resources. The amalgamation may also reduce the number of supervisors needed, so that some may be retrained or transferred to other departments. Alternatively, the supervisory span of control may be reduced, which may be an advantage where the supervisor acts as a 'resource person', but can lead to much tighter supervision of subordinates in a traditional environment.

There may also be a reduction in the number of levels in the hierarchy, usually when fewer people are employed. This is especially noticeable when the computer takes over the control and checking functions, which were previously done by people in a specific level of the hierarchy. For example, a banking computer system usually dramatically reduces the amount of work required of the middle levels in the staff hierarchy of the branches. Their previous function of checking transactions and controlling the work may be largely done by the computer, and the branch adapts to a broadly two-tier structure of cashiers on the counter and senior managerial staff who deal with loans, investments and professional banking work. This polarisation of abilities and job content tends to greatly reduce the flexibility and variety of work within the branches, as well as limiting the promotion opportunities for junior staff.

Control systems and centralisation

The other impact of computer technology is on the control systems of organisation and the degree of centralisation. The control system is concerned with the regulation of individuals, groups and technology towards achieving the objectives of the organisation. The basis of the control system is, of course, information about activities taking place within the organisation, which enables them to be co-ordinated and decisions to be made. In most complex organisations, the amount of information available and the range of variables to be considered are too vast for even the most intelligent person to cope with satisfactorily. It is here that the capacity of the computer to deal with enormous quantities of data quickly and easily is most valuable. Computer systems are essentially an information technology, providing an extension to man's brain power and thinking abilities, to assist in regulating and co-ordinating the tasks of many departments. Inevitably, the computer system becomes inextricably linked with the control system of the organisation in its role of processing all the information necessary for these activities. At the same time, the centralisation of control is often greatly increased, since the integration of widely differing kinds of information may be achieved through the use of a Management Information System. The result of using computer technology in this way is to concentrate organisational power and decision-making into fewer and fewer hands, by presenting information more concisely and extending the range of operations which each manager can control. Rapid feedback and a continuous critical appraisal of operations allow adjustments to be made quickly and considerably shortens the time required for planning.

A major difficulty with many existing computer-based systems is their size and pervasive nature. As experience with computer technology has grown, systems have tended to become larger and more extensive, at the same time as increasing the formalisation and centralisation of routines and control procedures. They represent a massive investment in terms of time and equipment and in the structural changes often made during their implementation. Naturally, organisations try to maintain a stable situation for as long as is needed to pay off this major investment. If, therefore, it becomes apparent that the system is not meeting the real needs of the organisation, because of design problems or unanticipated trends in the business environment, it is very difficult to make the necessary changes in the system and it takes on more and more the appearance of a muscle-bound wrestler, unable to cope with a situation for which it is no longer suited, yet too inflexible to adapt in the ways required. Large and inflexible computer-based systems seem to reinforce and exacerbate the problems of rigidity in the bureaucratic organisational structures, of which they have become a central core, in controlling the network of information.

Computer technology and the content of jobs

The corollary of these organisational impacts are the changes which have taken place in the job structures and work organisation of individual groups. However, there are considerable variations in the nature and degree of the impact according to the type of application being undertaken and the organisational characteristics. The effects may be summarised as follows

- jobs at lower levels tend to become more routine
- jobs at higher levels often become more interesting
- reduced control over timing and stricter deadlines
- procedures are specified in much greater detail
- quality standards are much tighter
- the role of the supervisor is very different

In considering whether or not computer systems and humanised work are compatible, it is important to look at the way jobs have been affected

Are Computer Systems and Humanised Work Compatible?

so far by computerisation. It will then be possible to look at ways of offsetting the detrimental effects and to suggest how the potential of computer systems may be used in positive and creative ways to achieve a better working environment.

One of the most noticeable effects of many computer systems is that they greatly reduce the discretion and autonomy exercised by individuals within the organisation, especially at lower levels. Significant areas of decision-making which was previously the responsibility of the individual may be taken over by the computer. The people may then be required to provide very detailed and specific information for the computer, but be excluded from actually taking decisions themselves. The result is often that the knowledge which has been built up over a long time may be programmed into the computer, leaving the individual simply as a by-stander. For example, a group of credit control clerks were asked to explain in precise detail how they made decisions on the credit-worthiness of customers. The knowledge was formalised into a computer programme, leaving the clerks to supply the information on the basis of which the computer accepted or rejected orders. Although the credit control was much tighter, the company lost many customers because the personal 'human' factors which the clerks also considered could not easily be programmed into the computer decision-making.

In another company, the jobs of order clerks consisted entirely of coding written orders coming from customers into numerical data for the computer, and they were required to be 100 per cent accurate. They lost their direct contact with customers and also much of their detailed knowledge of customer accounts.

The loss of personal contact with customers is often felt very keenly. From being able to see the pattern of transactions at a glance on a ledger card, many banking and accounting systems now store such data in a series of printouts, so there is no continuity of information about an account, and the personal reality is absorbed into a lengthy account number.

In other ways too, the skills and knowledge of people may be no longer needed. For example, numerically controlled machine tools can leave the skilled engineer watching while the machine performs precision operations. So too, the complex computer control systems being used in refineries, breweries and all types of process plants can lead to a dial-watching isolation for their operators. Williamson (1972) has pointed out that

We seem to be encouraging a ludicrous vision of industry where computers will do the decision-making, while men provide low-grade motive or brain power to carry out increasingly simple and repetitive tasks. A little reflection reveals the ultimate lunacy of such a proposition, and it can be recognised for what it is, a misuse of technology, and a misunderstanding of the proper functions of man and machine.

Where computer systems do not entirely replace established skills, they may require the job content to be so routine and structured that the work becomes very alienating. In particular, procedures are likely to be specified in much greater detail, even where the work involves dealing with queries rejected by the computer. The job may well consist of looking up reject codes in a procedures manual and then having the corrected data re-input for processing. It is also likely that the timing of the work will be much more closely regulated by the needs of the computer system. For example, a group of clerks had to meet a deadline of 2 pm for the day's work, so it could be punched and then processed by the computer during the evening. They got used to working flat out until 2 pm and then easing off during the afternoon.

The demands of most computer systems for very high quality standards are often difficult to meet and can be rather frustrating. Data must be correct even down to minute details, such as commas in the right place, and the exact spacing of characters. Whereas the human eye and brain would be tolerant of such details, the computer cannot cope, and so people are forced to conform to the rigorous standards required.

Computers contribute to improving work

However, it is also true that some systems have removed so much drudgery and routine work, that their users would under no circumstances wish to return to the previous situation, and greatly appreciate the freedom and opportunities for more interesting work which the computer affords them. This is especially the case for people at higher levels in organisations, and those more concerned with problem-solving. In these cases, the computer system can be an extremely valuable aid to the individual in doing his job, rather than a dominating feature of his work. For example, the jobs of senior staff and bank managers have become much more concerned with customer relations and new business opportunities, now that they can confidently leave much of the problem of accurate account updating to the computer. Airline booking systems have been improved dramatically and make the jobs of airline clerks and crew and travel agents much easier and far more

Are Computer Systems and Humanised Work Compatible?

efficient. The policeman on the beat can have vital information within seconds, so he can accomplish his work far more effectively and feel he has achieved something useful. Stock control systems have improved the information available to warehousemen so much that they can readily get a clear picture of stocks and feel that they are in much better control of supplies.

In some cases too the role of supervisors can be very different. For example, the control previously exercised by the supervisor over procedures, training and quality standards may well be taken over by the demands of the computer system. From spending time 'pushing the work through', the supervisor may become more concerned with acting as a resource person to his subordinates, in helping them to deal with queries and sort out problems. The previous tasks of giving instructions and providing feedback may also be largely done by the computer system rather than the supervisor. Sometimes this can be valuable, particularly where the computer points out errors rather than the supervisor, but both parties may feel their freedom is considerably curtailed by the system.

Whether individuals experience the effects of computer systems as dehumanising or not will depend also on their own personal needs and values. A person seeking interesting, challenging work is likely to feel more frustrated if his job becomes more routine and controlled, than someone who is quite happy doing a simple repetitive task which requires little thought. Equally, if a computer system takes away the routine drudgery from a job and provides the individual with more information to make all the difficult 'human' decisions, some people may feel overwhelmed by this increase in their degree of responsibility and long for the pre-computer days when simple ignorance was bliss.

The neutrality of computer systems

To discuss the impact of computer-based systems on organisational structures and work organisation implies that there is something inevitable about the matter. As if the introduction of a particular type of computer system must inexorably lead to a particular work organisation and specific effects on the content of jobs. Yet the very range and variation of the applications implemented so far, illustrate the fact that computer technology is the most versatile and flexible technology yet created by man. As Hedberg (1973) has pointed out

> the existence of a resource means typically that alternatives are available. There are alternative computer systems as well as there are

alternative futures ... The development is not deterministic. The technology in itself is neutral.

The fact that there is a tendency to consider that the effects of computer technology are deterministic, reflects the way it has been used, rather than any properties inherent in the technology. Computer-based systems are themselves neutral. They can only do what they have been set up and programmed to do by the system designers. At the same time computer systems provide the potential for creating far-reaching changes in our society, whose full implications we hardly yet realise. But whether the effects of such systems will be good or bad will depend largely on decisions which are made about the design and use of the powerful facilities they offer. The decisions made by the systems designers depend, of course, to a great extent on the personal values they hold. And if they are more concerned with the values of technology than the values of human development, then the computer-based systems they design may be technically elegant, but fail to fulfil the needs of people for satisfying 'humanised' work.

The distinction between the two types of value systems has been neatly summarised by Pirsig (1974) as romantic understanding and classical understanding. He says

> The romantic mode is primarily inspirational, imaginitive, creative, intuitive. Feelings rather than facts predominate. It does not proceed by reason or by laws. It proceeds by feeling intuition and esthetic conscience ... The classic mode, by contrast, proceeds by reason and by laws — which are themselves underlying forms of thought and behaviour. The classic style is straightforward, unadorned, unemotional, economical and carefully proportioned. Its purpose is not to inspire emotionally, but to bring order out of chaos and make the unknown known. It is not an esthetically free and natural style. It is esthetically restrained. Everything is under control. Its value is measured in terms of the skill with which this control is maintained.

The values of systems designers

In the past computer-based systems have been designed using concepts and values very similar to those which inspired industrial engineers to believe that they should define and control work so carefully that people would not be able to interfere with the smooth running of the machines. To achieve the maximum possible use of the technology,

Are Computer Systems and Humanised Work Compatible?

people were to be trained and given incentives which would enable them to adapt to the requirements dictated by the machine. The needs of people for interesting and challenging work were a very low priority, if needed they were even considered at all, except by accident or as a result of pressure from organised labour.

As Cherns (1973) pointed out

> The more sophisticated the production system, the more important the assumptions of its designers. With a comparatively simple system, the ingenuity of its operators can find a way to correct the designers' worst mistakes. Unauthorised modifications are easy to make to looms; but intolerable, if not impossible to make, to radar control systems. With large areas of organisation design under the effective control of systems analysts and computer programmers, the workers are impotent to alter their situation. And since the aim of industrial engineers, systems analysts and most management consultants is to eliminate as far as possible the effects of man's innate unpredictableness, all their products are designed to control and constrain human behaviour.

The value assumptions of the designer are embodied in the system, through the decisions he has made, based on his own model of the user and that of other groups, influencial in the decision process. The design of any system implies a model of the user and how he will operate that system. But the designer's model is not necessarily similar to that which the user has of himself. Indeed, it is very unlikely that the two models will coincide, since the background, training and objectives of the two parties are almost certain to be very different.

Hedberg and Mumford (1974) in their study of the values held by systems designers, argue that many of them appear to 'work from a position of technical optimism combined with a compliance model of men', that is, they try to maximise the use of the technology, while believing that human beings can be manipulated to accept virtually any system which does not contravene their personal value systems too grossly. By contrast, the system user is developing a personal self-actualising model of himself and will soon reject technological change which contravenes this. One often hears systems designers speak about 'selling the system to the user' and setting up training and consultation programmes to gain user acceptance and avoid the bogey of 'resistance to change', without any real intention that the user's own ideas should influence the design of the system with which he will work.

The values and objectives of management

It is not only the value decisions of the systems designers which need to be examined and hopefully enlightened by new training courses. To a large extent, they are constrained by the objectives set out for new systems by the senior management of the organisation. Just as systems designers make value decisions based on their own personal 'models of man', so managers too set objectives and take decisions based on their models of the business environment and future trends. It may be that they are experiencing some problems and they see the new computer system as a means of alleviating the problem to some extent.

For example, an organisation which was finding great difficulty in recruiting the calibre of staff required because of a very tight labour market situation, decided to design and implement a major computer-based system which could be successfully operated by people with very much lower qualifications. By the time this major system had been designed and implemented, the labour market situation had eased a great deal, and it became possible once more to recruit the kind of people they really felt they needed. The personnel department joyfully continued their earlier recruitment policy, only to find that the staff soon became bored, operating a system designed with other users in mind.

In another organisation, a computer system was introduced to cope with a large and increasing volume of business. Unfortunately, the demand altered a few years later in favour of a type of business for which this system was very largely unsuitable, but into which the company felt they had to move in order to remain competitive. This required further investment in different computing facilities, before the original costs had been written off, as well as considerable retraining of staff.

The feasibility of introducing a computer system is usually determined on the basis of cost/benefit analyses which take very little account of social costs and benefit in achieving the required objectives. It is unusual for these overall objectives to suggest that the occasion of the introduction of a computer-based system is a time to try and make positive attempts to improve jobs and the work organisation. If any explicit social objectives are set at all, it is usually in terms of reducing the number of people involved, with the minimum of retraining and disturbance, in the shortest possible time.

Society bears the cost

The cost of designing systems from such narrow economic and technical concepts in terms of individual boredom and alienation, disturbed family relationships and mental health problems, is not borne by the organisations operating the systems creating these problems. They may well suffer some of the costs, in the form of turnover, absenteeism and other 'counter-productive' activities. But individuals, families and society as a whole must bear the balance of the costs, without having the option or perhaps even being fully aware of the source from which such costs emanate. Indeed, the cumulative effect may be to take society in directions which it would neither wish to go, nor which are in its best interests.

However, there are now signs that the realisation is slowly dawning that the design philosophies of the past were inadequate. The pressure for change is coming not only from individuals and groups of workers, but trade unions are also beginning to exert influence on their behalf, especially in West Germany (Leminsky 1974). For example, they are working to ensure that

- the training of systems designers deals with social problems
- unions, works councils and shop stewards are consulted at all stages of the planning process
- personnel and social planning is integrated into management philosophy.

Computer specialists themselves have become very concerned about the effects of systems on people and their jobs. Indeed, the training courses which are now being run for systems designers are beginning to devote a much greater proportion of time to understanding the organisational context into which systems will be introduced, and the needs and expectations of the people who will use such systems. Courses in organisational behaviour, sociology and psychology are now being included and related to the technical problems of designing computer-based systems, so that the interplay between the social and technical aspects of the systems can be clearly seen, and a more proper balance achieved between them.

This growing awareness is being supported by computer manufacturers themselves. For example, guidelines drawn up for the Association for Computing Machinery (Sterling 1974) point out

The 'utility' of humanising procedures is not apparent from cost/ benefit calculations but arises from the point of view of the quality of life — not only of our own but also of future generations who will be saddled with the systems which are designed and implemented today. The wish to keep these systems humane and dignifying must take its place with the desire to keep the air breathable and the water drinkable as a necessary counter motive to the drive of government and industry to be as efficient and cost-conscious as possible.

Of course, computer-based systems must be economically viable and efficient, but it is essential to try and develop an appreciation among both systems designers and managers that it is possible to reach these objectives, at the same time as achieving the worthwhile social objectives of more interesting and satisfying work.

A new philosophy is needed

It seems clear that a new philosophy and logic is urgently needed, both in the board room and the computer systems department, to begin to tackle the problems which have emerged during the rapid development of computer technology. Problems also occur when organisations find that computer systems, structured using the bureaucratic model, based on the principle of vertical control, are mismatched with the need to react quickly in a rapidly changing environment. Long-term trends too are rendering the logic of bureaucratic structures obsolete. Bennis (1966) has argued that bureaucracy is in decline and has forecast the changes he believes will take place during the next 25 years. He predicts that technology will develop rapidly, as will the value systems of society. People will receive better education and will tend to increase their rate of movement between jobs. In turn, their attitudes towards work will change, in that people will become more intellectually committed to their jobs and demand more involvement, participation and autonomy in their work. At the same time, the tasks of the firm will become more technical, unprogrammed and too complicated for one person to handle or for individual supervision. To cope with these factors, a new type of social structure will develop, which will consist of adaptive, changing, 'temporary' groups brought together to solve specific problems. The group members will be differentiated, not vertically according to rank and role, but flexibly according to skill and professional training. Bennis considers that this type of structure should increase motivation and therefore effectiveness, because of the satisfactions intrinsic to the task. He concludes that 'there is a congruence between the educated individual's need for meaningful, satisfactory and creative tasks and flexible structure or autonomy'.

If changing trends bear out the predictions which Bennis has made, and there are clear signs of a movement in this direction, then it is essential that early consideration is given to the role which computer-based systems will play. If future systems are designed along rigid and bureaucratic lines, then they are likely to conflict with the need for flexible, adaptive organisational structures. Given also that computer-based systems tend to hold structures stable for rather long periods of time, they could retard the pace at which such changes can take place, so creating further turbulence. On the other hand, if systems designers become sufficiently aware of the changing values and the desire of people for jobs which are challenging and motivating, then future computer-based systems may in fact support and encourage the trend away from bureaucracy rather than conflicting with it.

Decentralised and non-hierarchical systems

But many systems designers may argue that they have already realised the potential of computer systems for decentralising the work and decision-making of an organisation. For example, the use of on-line facilities from remote terminals may be used to decentralise the task of data preparation, and allow the initiators of information to have direct access to the computer. Decentralised enquiry facilities may also enable decisions to be made at the point they arise, rather than having to be taken at some centralised information point. And there is no doubt that using advanced computer technology in these ways can greatly improve the jobs which people do and give them greater control and involvement with their own work, while having available the powerful facilities offered by the computer.

It is important to recognise that management values are crucial in such situations. For some computer systems which provide for decentralised decision-making could also be used for centralised control. But the way in which the neutral technology is used depends on the values of its designers and managers. As Herbst (1976) has pointed out

> In the case of bureaucratic hierarchical organisations, an attempt to move out of this system may be perceived as going in the direction of the opposite, that is, a chaotic unstructured state. Alternatively, transition from, say, a centralised to a decentralised system produces the converse without necessarily changing the basic mode of operation of the organisation. ... The process of social change can become locked within and unable to go beyond the inherent organisational logic.

He suggests that if the basic assumption of each member being restricted to a single specialised task is abandoned, then the requirement for bureaucratic, hierarchical structures will disappear and be replaced by organisations which have the capacity for multistructured functioning. Three types of non-hierarchical alternatives can be identified, namely, the composite autonomous group, the matrix group and the network group. Examples of each of these types of organisation have existed for some time, but have generally been unrecognised or exceptional because they are only on a small scale.

'Humanised' computer-based systems

However, there are already examples of computer-based systems which have been designed based on concepts very different from those normally used. Here, systems designers have appreciated the inherent flexibility of computer-technology and consciously set the objective of using the change to a new system as an opportunity for creating more challenging work. An excellent practical illustration of this approach is the computer system described by Paul Hill (1971) installed at Shell's refinery at Teesport to carry out much of the data logging and plant control operations normally done by operators in the older established refineries. The computer-operator interface was seen as a critical factor for the effective operation of the refinery, to make the best match between the capabilities of the men and the machine. This was particularly important since operators needed to be able to handle information quickly and effectively, given the very high level of instrumentation and automation on the plant. From a purely technical point of view, the designers could have decided to maximise the use of the computer's capabilities by closing as many information and control loops as possible, so the need for intervention by the operator was reduced to a minimum. However, they were concerned that the operator's role, in being confined largely to monitoring the performance of the computer, would not be challenging enough, nor involve him sufficiently with the on-going process of control. In setting up the computer-operator interface the company

> decided therefore that a balance had to be struck between what was technically feasible, on the one hand, and what was necessary, on the other, to create a role for the operator that would enable him to become internally motivated to perform his task effectively. This meant that certain loops which could technically have been closed, were passed instead, as it were, through the operator, so that he

could exert his influence and become part of the control process. The role of the computer was accordingly seen as the logging of data, the automatic control of certain variables, and the rapid provision of information on which the operator or supervisor could take better decisions about the control of other process variables.

Designing the computer in this way to include the operator, fitted in well with the wish to design challenging jobs. Each operator was given the scope to be highly flexible and had the opportunity of doing up to seven different jobs, within the shift team in which he worked on the refinery.

Another interesting example of the way in which computer systems may be designed to support non-bureaucratic forms of organisation is the quality control information system which Volvo have designed for their advanced car assembly plant at Kalmar in Sweden. The factory functions are co-ordinated by means of a system using four computers, which compiles, processes and provides information on aspects of quality. The system makes possible decentralisation and delegation of jobs by giving operators a great amount of responsibility for quality inspection work. The Volvo Report (1975) explains

> An important job for the computer is to quickly relay information on quality and operating performance on the cars each group has worked on ... Information from the special control stations along the production chain is continuously fed back on video screens. The group thus learns immediately if their work is showing poor results further along the chain and they can therefore correct their working methods.

However, the system is also designed to provide information when specially good results have been attained, thus providing positive feedback to the operators. The Kalmar computer system is a good illustration of integration between the technical system and the human work organisation to provide information and assistance to assembly teams in achieving a high level of quality in their output.

The example of 'humanised' computer-based systems at Shell and Volvo are, of course, rather ambitious, and were made possible because completely new plants were being established. There was a determination from the start on the part of both management and systems designers that they would use the opportunity to find ways of creating a balance between the facilities offered by advanced computer technology and the work needs of the operators. However, the same determination and willingness to consider alternatives can achieve exciting results in systems of a much smaller scale, using computers for very different purposes.

Participative design processes

These changing attitudes were reflected in the design process of an on-line sales order processing system introduced by TAC Ltd, a division of the Turner & Newall Group. The system was to replace an earlier batch processing system dealing with sales ledger, order processing, invoicing and finished goods stock recording. The terms of reference for the project included the specific objective '. . . to increase the job satisfaction of the clerks employed in the order processing offices and to significantly involve them in the development of the new system.' This approach marked a considerable break with the design procedure for earlier computer systems, since rather than systems analysts working out the technical and human alternatives of the new system and then discussing them with users and obtaining agreement, the sales clerks themselves were encouraged to play a major role in analysing their own problems and needs and producing a new form of work organisation incorporating the computer-based system. Their analysis clearly highlighted the fact that the existing work organisation had created two very different types of work, namely the very routine, boring task of preparing data for punching and a highly stressful task of dealing with queries and complaints from customers. The new on-line system gave the clerks the opportunity to control their own data input directly to the computer through visual display units. However, they felt that the 'technically optimal' organisation of having full-time specialist VDU operators would perpetuate the problems of the two distinct working groups. Instead, the clerks created a work organisation in which small groups were responsible for dealing with all the orders for a specific geographical area, and each group was allocated a VDU for its own data input. Within the group, individual tended to look after particular customer accounts, but they maintained a high degree of flexibility in coping with orders coming in, customers queries and data input and order progressing using the VDU.

Advances in computer technology

The upgrading from off-line batch processing computer systems to on-line time sharing, has made it technically possible to design systems which provide the initiators of data with immediate access to the

Are Computer Systems and Humanised Work Compatible?

computer, while at the same time enabling them to retain control and keep in touch with the information, rather than releasing control to a specialised computer department. This advance in technology has complemented the growing awareness of the needs of people for interesting and stimulating tasks and for greater control and involvement with their own work. However, both off-line and on-line types of computer systems are highly centralised, though as we have seen, a large measure of decentralisation may be achieved by enabling people to take decisions on the basis of information provided by remote terminals. Nevertheless, such centralised computer systems inevitably reflect and support the centralised bureaucratic structures of many organisations, and indeed have, in many cases, created an even greater degree of centralisation than existed before computerisation.

Now, however, an alternative possibility is becoming realistic and is likely to expand rapidly in the future. With the advent of the fourth generation of computer systems, a new style of computing is becoming widespread, namely distributed computing, and this is likely to make the extension of non-hierarchical forms of work organisation much more feasible and indeed desirable than would have been thought possible only a few years ago. Technological developments have now made it practicable to create systems which make use of small, autonomous mini-computer systems capable of handling all the information for a working group. These 'distributed' computing systems are very different from the centralised computer systems of earlier generations, which required very expensive machinery and specialised staff working in an air-conditioned environment. For example, the hardware is very much cheaper, making use of large scale integrated circuits (LSI) for processing and 'floppy discs' for the storage of information, both of which are inexpensive and reliable. Mini-computers can also be operated by non-specialist staff, and can work reliably in an ordinary office environment.

The potential of the development of distributed computer systems for supporting and complementing non-hierarchical forms of work organisation can readily be appreciated. The concept and operation of, for example, an autonomous working group becomes a very different proposition if that group can make use of its own autonomous mini-computer system, rather than linking directly to a centralised computer system whose design may be based on bureaucratic value assumptions. Equally, the fact that distributed computer systems have lowered the cost of information processing so much and are so reliable, makes them very attractive on cost grounds alone, and therefore likely to be widely adopted in the future by cost-conscious managements, with little concern for achieving social objectives. We may therefore shortly have the spectacle of computer systems, selected on economic and technical grounds, being ideally suited to the organisational structures which not only permit, but also support the development of individual and group autonomy.

Conclusion

It may then be that computer technology has come a full circle. From its early days, when computer-based systems tended to reduce people to the level of slaves to the machine and systems designers tried to minimise the extent of 'unreliable' human intervention, we may now be moving to a very different situation. The exciting technological developments which have taken place over the past few years will mean that future computer systems will have very different characteristics from those to which we have become accustomed. These changes will take place independently of any efforts which may be made to create more satisfying work. As Grosch (1974) has pointed out 'Major and worthwhile changes in processor and memory components are certain and striking new systems architecture is probable; the latter will be in response to marketing considerations.' At the same time the improved hardware offers much greater flexibility and potential to design systems which will be better suited to human needs. While the new generation of computers is a technological breakthrough in itself, an equally dramatic breakthrough is in the changing perceptions of the ways in which these major advances may be applied.

For significant changes are taking place in the attitudes and values of systems designers, towards the realisation that systems can and should use full potential of the people operating the system. Conferences, training courses and increasing knowledge and experience are gradually making computer specialists aware of their crucial role in the design and overall planning process of organisations. They are no longer just technicians, translating these processes into computer-based information systems, but they have become organisation designers themselves, with tremendous responsibility, not only for the future of their own organisations, but for the future of society as a whole.

It is imperative that these trends should gain momentum quickly, to offset the traditional values which presently pervade our organisations and which threaten to overwhelm them. Systems of technology and administration have become so overcomplicated that their futures could very easily pose a threat to the value systems of democracy and humanisation, even as these are gaining ground. The principle formulated by Speiser (1972) following the New York black-out may become very important in future development:

> In systems of a high degree of complexity, there can occur conditions of instability, even under perfectly normal operating circumsances, in which an almost arbitrarily small perturbation can have catastrophic effects.

But computers have become such an integral part of our civilisation that we are now facing the challenge of the ultimate contradiction, posed by Zemanek (1974):

> While human properties and values are in danger of being destroyed by the physical and technical mentality, the protection of the individual and of human society can be achieved only by the methods and tools provided by science and technology.

Only by recognising and coping with this challenge can we ensure that computer-based systems and humanised work are indeed compatible.

References

Bennis, W., *Beyond Bureaucracy* (McGraw-Hill, New York, 1966).
Burns, T. and Stalker, G., *The Management of Innovation* (Tavistock Publications, London, 1961).
Cherns, A., 'Better Working Lines — a Social Scientist's View', *Occupational Psychology*, Vol. 47 (1973) pp. 23-8.
Crozier, M., *The Bureaucratic Phenomenon* (University of Chicago Press, Chicago, 1964).
Gouldner, A.W., *Patterns of Industrial Bureaucracy* (The Free Press, Glencoe, 1954).
Grosch, H.R.J., 'Development trends and Economic Aspects' in Proceedings Vol. 11. 1B1 1CC., International Symposium on the Economics of Informatics, Mainz, September 1974.
Hedberg, B., 'Computer Systems and the Quality of Working Life', Preprint 1/73-26 (International Institute of Management, Berlin, May 1973).
Hedberg, B. and Mumford, E., 'The Design of Computer Systems: man's vision of man as an integral part of the system design process', in E. Mumford and H. Sackman (eds.), *Human Choice and Computers* (North-Holland, Amsterdam, 1975).
Herbst, P., *Alternatives to Hierarchies* (Martinus Nijhoff, 1976).
Hill, P., *Towards a new philosophy of Management* (Gower Press, Essex, 1971).
Leminskey, G., 'Humanisation of work in the FRG', in E. Mumford and H.

Sackman (eds.), *Human Choice and Computers* (North-Holland, Amsterdam, 1975).

Lindholm, R. and Norstedt, J., *The Volvo Report* (Swedish Employers' Confederation, 1975).

Pirsig, R.M., *Zen and the Art of Motorcycle Maintenance* (The Bodley Head, London, 1974).

Speiser, A.P., 'Computers and Technology' in H. Zemanek (ed.), *The Skyline of Information Processing*, Proceedings of the 10th Anniversary Celebration of I.F.I.P. (North-Holland, Amsterdam, 1972).

Sterling, T.D., 'Guidelines for Humanising Computerised Information Systems', *Communications of the Association for Computing Machinery* (November, 1974) pp. 609-13.

Weber, M., *The Theory of Social and Economic Organisation* translated by A.M. Henderson and Talcott Parsons (Oxford University Press, New York, 1947).

Whisler, T., *The Impact of Computers on Organisations* (Praeger Publishers, New York, 1970).

Williamson, D.T.N., 'The Anachronistic Factory', Proceedings of the Royal Society, A331 (1972) pp. 139-60.

Zemanek, H., 'The Human Being and the Automation: Selected aspects of a philosophy of information processing' in E. Mumford and H. Sackman (eds.), *Human Choice and Computers* (North-Holland, Amsterdam, 1975).

4 TAYLOR IN THE OFFICE
Michael J.E. Cooley

Introduction

Pronouncements on the dehumanisation of work in so-called technologically advanced societies have tended to concentrate on manual tasks. That this should be so is not surprising. Opression in the factory is now so great as to be counter-productive. In addition to our well known problems in Great Britain, we learn of the 18 per cent absentee rate at Fiat in Italy. Recently Sweden has felt the necessity to introduce protective workshops introduced, incidentally, to protect people from the advanced technology which we had always been given to understand would liberate human beings from soul destroying, back breaking tasks, and free them to engage in more creative work. Along with these examples, the sabotage of products at the General Motors plant in Lordstown, Ohio, reveals but the tip of a great iceberg of seething industrial discontent.

Less spectacular, but even more significant as indicators, are the ever increasing rate of production defects and errors, the widespread increase in accidents, absenteeism and turnover, and the very real difficulty, in spite of the bait of a financial anaesthetic, of finding adequate workers to submit to the degradation of the modern factory. Even when the employer does succeed in finding sufficient 'human machine appendages', his problems are by no means at an end. The industrial worker, despite a class ridden educational system which systematically seeks to reduce his or her expectations to an absolute minimum, and despite the continuous bludgeoning by the mass media, still retains a degree of dignity and initiative which employers find alarming. Indeed, it is one of the greatest tributes to human dignity that the industrial worker obstinately refuses to meet the specification 'That he should be so stupid and so phlegmatic that he more nearly resembles in his mental make-up, the ox than any other type' (Taylor, 1947). It is therefore not surprising that human beings, when viewed in this way and required to work within a productive process which treats them as oxen, should take what steps they can, however defensive, to assert their humanity. These attempts are not unrelated to the failure rate in parts of industry which have reached such proportions that half the equipment lies idle in General Motors' most modern factory — where the intensity and monotony of work surpasses anything previously imposed on assembly line workers (Gorz, 1976).

Faced with this massive and growing contradiction, employers are seeking aid from a whole host of 'Hawthorne agents' such as job enrichment specialists, group technologists and industrial psychologists. The industrial reality is that these 'agents' in no way change the basic power relationships which give rise to these contradictions in the first instance. It is, as a Lucas shop steward once put it, 'like keeping people in a cage and having a long debate about the colour of the bars'.

Against this background, it is not surprising that in the community at large there is a growing, if as yet embryonic, realisation of the social and economic costs of the 'efficient factory' in terms of structural unemployment, frantic energy consumption, lack of job satisfaction and the squandering of our most precious asset — peoples' talent and ingenuity. While we may not be quite sure how small is actually beautiful, there can be little doubt that the 'efficiency' of the factory system will be more and more questioned.

Fixed capital as a dehumaniser

Due to inflexibility, total disregard for societal aspirations, and blindness to the inherent destructiveness of capitalist forms of production (even in the so-called socialist countries) employers seem determined to repeat all the mistakes in the field of white collar work that they have already made at such tremendous cost in the field of manual work. If therefore, steps are to be taken to prevent the inevitable dehumanisation of intellectual work, it will be necessary to attempt to define the nature of the dehumanisation elements for white collar workers. Such a definition would also help in the long term to undo the damage that has been done in the field of manual work. To develop such a definition, it is necessary to examine the contradictions which arise when any form of work is subjected to a technological change in which the organic composition of capital is changed. By that one means when the production process becomes capital intensive rather than labour intensive. This is so because white collar workers, those who do intellectual work, are less necessary in capital intensive offices.

There is now a widespread feeling among both hand and brain workers that the more elaborate and scientific the equipment they design and build, the more they become subordinated to it — that is to the objects of their own labour. The more sophisticated production becomes, the more dehumanised the labour process becomes. This can only be understood when seen in the historical and economic context of technological change as a whole. The use of fixed capital, i.e. machinery, and in the case of intellectual workers, computers, in the productive process marks a fundamental change in the mode of production. It cannot be viewed merely as an increase in the rate at which tools are used to work on raw materials. The hand tool was entirely animated by the worker, and the rate at which the commodity was produced and the quality of that commodity depended (apart from raw materials, market forces and supervision) on the strength, tenacity, dexterity and ingenuity of the worker. With fixed capital it is quite the contrary in that the method of work is transformed as regards its use value (material existence) into that form most suitable for fixed capital. The scientific knowledge which predetermines the speeds and feeds of the machine and the sequential movements of its inanimate parts, the mathematics used in compiling Numerically Controlled Programmes do not exist in the consciousness of the operator. They are external to him or her and act upon him or her through the machine as an alien force.

The same is true of the intellectual working in a computerised or highly synchronised environment. Thus science, as it manifests itself to him through fixed capital, although it is merely the accumulation of knowledge and skill now appropriated, confronts him as an alien and hostile force and further subordinates him to the machine. The nature of his activity, the movement of his limbs, the rate and sequence of these movements are predetermined in quite minute detail by the 'scientific' requirements of the fixed capital. Likewise, the decision-making processes of the intellectual worker are also constrained by the nature of the computerised programmes that are available to him. Thus, objectivised labour, whether by hand or brain, in the form of fixed capital emerges in the productive process as a dominating force opposed to living labour. Fixed capital represents not only the appropriation of living labour, but in its sophisticated forms (computer hardware and software) appropriates the scientific and intellectual output of white collar workers, and his own intellect opposes him as an alien force (Cooley 1972). Therefore, the more a worker puts into the object of his labour, the less there is left of himself. For example, the welder at General Motors who takes a robotic welding device and guides its probes through the welding process of a car body is on the one hand building skill into the machine and on the other de-skilling himself. The accumulation of welding experience is absorbed by the robot's self-programming system and will never be forgotten. Similarly, a mathematician working as a stressman in an aircraft company may design a software package for the stress analysis of aircraft structures and suffer the same consequence in his job. In each case they have given part of themselves to the machine, and in so doing conferred life on the subject of their labour, but now this life no longer belongs to them but to the owner of the object.

Since the product of his labour does not belong to the worker, but to the owner of the means of production in whose service the work is done and for whose benefit the product of labour is produced, it necessarily follows that the object of the workers' labour confronts him as an alien and hostile force since it is used not in his interest, but in the interest of the owner of the means of production. Thus the 'loss of self' of the worker is but a manifestation of the fundamental contradictions at the economic base of our society. It is a reflection of the antagonistic contradiction between the interests of capital and the interests of labour. Fixed capital, therefore, at this stage in history is the embodiment of a contradiction; namely, that the means which could make possible the liberation of the worker from routine, soul destroying tasks is simultaneously the means of his own enslavement.

In summary then, firstly, we can say that the humanisation of work is intimately bound up with the ownership of the means of production. A change in ownership in this sense does not mean the transfer of economic power from one small elite to another. It is clear that a production line in the Soviet Union is no more enriching for a worker than one in Detroit. Secondly, any serious consideration of the humanisation of work must bring into question the underlying assumptions of science and technology as practised in our so called technologically advanced societies. In the past it has been widely assumed that science, because of its objectivity, must be neutral. It was thought that science could serve any kind of society. More recently, this assumption has been questioned (Rose, 1972). It is quite conceivable that our scientific methodology, and in particular our design methodology, has been distorted by the social forces which have given rise to its development. Science may well have built into its methodology a wide range of political and ideological assumptions that embody notions of efficiency which are by their nature dehumanising (Dickson, 1974).

It is fairly self evident that those who are seriously concerned about the dehumanisation of work, as distinct from a little window dressing, will have to look very critically at the 'scientific' principles involved in machine design. It is encouraging to see that at least one or two leading technologists are beginning to do so (Rosenbrock, 1975).

Synchronised/computerised response to fixed capital

Another important obstacle to the humanisation of work, is the increasing rate of obsolescence of equipment (the increasingly short life of fixed capital). Sophisticated equipment is now obsolete in about three years. In addition, the investment cost of the means of production (as distinct from the price of individual commodities) is ever increasing. Confronted, therefore, with equipment which is getting obsolete literally by the minute and requirements of enormous capital investment, employers will seek to exploit it 24 hours a day. This trend has long been evident on the shop floor, and the effects of shift working are already well documented (Mott, 1965). The same problems are now beginning to be quite evident in the field of white collar work. Five years ago, the AUEW (TASS) was involved in a major dispute with Rolls Royce which cost the union one quarter of a million pounds. The company sought, among other things, to impose on the design staff at its Bristol plant, the following conditions:

> The acceptance of shift work in order to exploit high capital equipment.
>
> The acceptance of work measurement techniques.
>
> The division of work into basic elements and the setting of times for these elements, such times to be compared with actual performance.

In this particular case industrial action prevented the company from imposing these conditions. They are, however, the sort of conditions that employers will increasingly seek to impose on their white collar workers. When staff workers, whether they be technical, administrative, or clerical, work in a highly synchronised computerised environment, the employer will seek to ensure that each element of their work is ready to feed into the process at the precise time at which it is required. A mathematician for example, will find that he has to have calculations ready in the same way a Ford worker has to have the wheel ready for the car as it passes him on the production line. Consequently, we can say that as more technological change and computerisation enters into white collar areas, the more workers in those areas will become proletarianised. The consequences of shift work spread across the family, social and cultural life of the white collar worker. In a survey carried out in West Germany it was demonstrated that the ulcer rate of workers on a rotating shift was eight times higher than among other workers. Other surveys have shown that the divorce rate among shift workers is approximately 50 per cent higher than the average, and that the juvenile delinquency rate of their children can often be 80 per cent higher. Thus in practice, far from humanising the nature of work, there are grounds already for suggesting that in the field of white collar work, high capital equipment is diminishing the quality of life of intellectual workers just as it has already done on the shop floor.

In the man/machine interaction, man is the dialectical opposite of the machine, in that he is slow, inconsistent, unreliable and highly creative. The machine is the opposite, in that it is fast, consistent, reliable and totally non-creative. Superficially, it would appear that this provides for the perfect man/machine symbiosis. In practice, the reverse is the case. The computer can produce quantitative data at an incredible rate. As the intellectual worker tries to keep abreast of this and also cope with the qualitative elements, the stress upon him or her can be truly enormous. In the fields of intellectual work examined by the AUEW, some instances were found where the decision-making rate is forced up by approximately 1900 per cent (Cooley, 1973). Clearly, human beings cannot stand this pace of interaction for long. Experiments show that the design efficiency of an engineer working at a visual display unit decreases by 30 to 40 per cent in the first hour, and 70 to 80 per cent in the second hour (Bernholz, 1973). Since employers, particularly in non-university environments, will expect the equipment to be used continuously, the situation can be extremely stressful. Indeed, the International Labour Office (1975) has recommended safeguards against the nervous fatigue of white collar workers. Also, an International Federation of Information Processing working party recently suggested that mental hazards 'caused by inhumanely designed computer systems should be considered a punishable offence just as endangering the bodily safety' (IFIP 1974). Thus what might be a delightfully stimulating plaything for the systems designer may be the basis for a dehumanised work environment for the user (Kling, 1973).

The literature dealing with the visual fatigue of intellectual workers on visual display units, particularly when handling alphanumerical data, is extensive and of long standing. Indeed, some continental trade unions have already investigated these problems and are specifying rest periods and other safeguards (Cooley 1976). Far more important would be to insist upon the redesign of the equipment.

Fragmented work as a dehumaniser

Central to the dehumanisation of work in the intellectual field, just as in the field of manual work, is the fragmentation of work into narrow alienated tasks, each minutely timed. This fragmentation is, of course, absolutely 'rational' if you regard people as mere units of production and are concerned solely with maximising the profit you can extract from them. Indeed, viewed from that premise, it is not merely rational but also scientific. In fact to reduce the worker to a blind unthinking appendage of the machine is the very essence of Scientific Management. Paradoxically, Taylor's Scientific Management on the shop floor initially increased the intellectual activity of the staff in offices. Taylor (1947) himself explained that his system

> is aimed at establishing a clear cut and novel division of mental and manual work throughout the workshops. It is based upon the precise time and motion study of each workers' job in isolation, and relegates the entire mental parts of the task in hand to the managerial staff.

Sixty years of this scientific management has seen the fragmentation of work grind through the spectrum of workshop activity engulfing even the most creative and satisfying manual jobs (such as toolmaking). Throughout that period, most industrial laboratories, design offices and administrative centres were the sanctuaries of the conceptual planning and administrative aspects of work. In those areas, one spur to output was a dedication to the task in hand, an interest in it, and a satisfaction of dealing with a job from start to finish. Some observers, including the writer, cautioned that this situation would soon be brought to an end as the monopolies, in their quest for increased profits would bring their 'rational and scientific' methods into these more self organising and comparatively easy going fields. The objective circumstances for this were already set when in some industries 50 or 60 per cent of those employed were scientific, technical and managerial staff. It was evident that the more science ceased to be an amateur gentleman's affair and was integrated into the productive processes, the more scientists and technologists would become part of the workforce itself. Indeed, it was even suggested that as high capital equipment, such as computers, became available to scientists and technologists, they would be paced by the machine, and eventually their intellectual activity would be divided into routine tasks, and work study used to set precise times for its synchronisation with the rest of the 'rational procedure'.

Some scientists and technologists, particularly those in the computer field, who look upon this view with derision, would be well advised to recall what the father of their industry, Charles Babbage (1832) had to say on the matter. Even in the 1830s he anticipated Taylorism in the field of intellectual work. In a chapter entitled, 'On The Division of Manual Labour', his message is clear

> We have already mentioned what may perhaps appear paradoxical to some of our readers, that the division of labour can be applied with equal success to mental as well as mechanical operations, and that it ensures in both the same economy of time.

In spite of these warnings, and in spite of strikes by some white collar unions against the use of the stopwatch in offices, these predictions were for the most part treated either as the scare mongering of slick trade union leaders keen on increasing their flock, or as a plain absurdity. 'That will be the day when someone tries to measure my intellectual activity' was a frequent reaction. Unfortunately, the day may be much closer than many would like to believe. In June 1974, 'A Classification and Terminology of Mental Work' appeared in *Workstudy*. It suggests that much 'progress' has been made in this direction. Having identified the hierarchy of physical work i.e., job, operation, element, therblig, it states

> The first three of these are general concepts — i.e., they can be applied equally well to physical or mental work. The last term, the therblig, is specific to physical work. All elements of physical work consist of a small number of basic physical motions first codified by Gilbreth (Therblig is an anagram of Gilbreth) and later amended by the American Society of Mechanical Engineers, and in the British Standard Glossary. The logical pattern would be complete if a similar breakdown of elements into basic mental motions — or Yalks — were available.

The paper describes in detail how to classify input yalks, output yalks and processing yalks. It describes how each of these can be subdivided into basic mental operations. It goes as far as to draw a division between the passive reception of visual signals (seeing) and the active reception (looking) as well as the passive reception of audio signals (hearing) and the active reception (listening). The paper implies that these techniques will be used in the more simple aspects of mental work. However, it concludes:

We have tried to show that mental work is a valid and practical field for the application of work study, that basic mental motions exist and can be identified and classified in a meaningful way provided one does not trespass too far into the more complex mental routines and processes. A set of basic mental motions have been identified, named, described and coded as a basis for future work measurement research leading to the compilation of standard times. There are good prospects that such times could play a valuable part in work study projects.

It is, however, clear that just as in the case of highly creative manual work, these techniques will 'trespass too far into the more complex mental routines and processes'. Whether one regards this type of research as pseudo-scientific or not, there can be little doubt about how it will be deployed. The employers of scientific, technical, and administrative staff, including some forms of managerial staff, will see it as a powerful form of psychological intimidation to mould their intellectual workers to the 'mental production line'. It is perhaps a recognition of this tactical importance which prompted Howard C. Carlson, a psychologist employed by General Motors, to say 'The Computer may be to middle management what the assembly line is to the hourly worker.'

The computer is used not only as a Trojan Horse for Taylorism in the field of management and scientific work, even the university is no longer a sanctuary for non-alienated work. The well known Frank Wolfe algorithm is now used to work out the actual work load for university lecturers, (Cooley, 1976). The wider socio-political effects on manual workers of working in a capital intensive environment, have been frequently described, (Kornhauser, 1965). The effects of mechanisation, automation and computerisation in the field of white collar work are likely to be equally great (Cooley, 1975). Automation increases the authoritarian control which an employer has over his employees and strengthens the hand of those who support a tougher attitude to their employees (Hoos, 1960). It has been suggested that the success of a computer system depends on the readiness of the users to 'let their behaviour be formalised' (Koeppe, 74), and that the computer 'disables and weakens the non-machine like behaviour' of the human being (Zemanek, 1974). By ignoring the socio-political assumptions of design methodology, we have

> failed to recognise as anti-human, and consequently to oppose, the effect of values built in to the apparatus, instrument, and machines

of their (Capitalist) technological system. So machines have played
the part of Trojan Horses in their relation to the Labour Movement.
Productivity becomes more important than fraternity, discipline
outweighs freedom. The product is in fact more important than the
producer — even in countries struggling for socialism. (My translation
— M.C.) (Jungk, 73).

However, high capital investment in equipment in the field of intellectual work not only carries these consequences with it, but it can lead directly to the ultimate dehumanisation of work, that is, the denial of any work at all. High capital equipment, as pointed out earlier, increases the organic composition of capital which becomes capital rather than labour intensive. In short, people are replaced by machines. Structural unemployment as distinct from cyclic unemployment is now widespread in the technologically advanced nations. The pronouncements of politicians and others indicate that this is likely to be of long duration. The traumatic experience of white collar workers who experience structural unemployment has to be seen to be believed. One Senior Design Engineer, a TASS member in North West London, used to creep out to 'work each day' at the normal time, and hide all day in a library, returning at normal finishing time rather than admit to his wife and children that he was out of a job. The employers have been planning for quite some time for structural unemployment among this level of employees. This is a tragic symptom of our times. Gomolak and Raithel (1974) say it is clear that even in West Germany, in spite of its 'economical miracle' there are employers who are carefully preparing for the present structural unemployment.

A fool's scenario

It is sometimes admitted that high capital equipment does indeed bring these problems in its wake, but that the overall advantages do outweigh the disadvantages. The technological fixers, the messenger boys of the large monopolies, have carefully contrived a scenario which elevates work to a new level where it is performed by the knowledge worker. This new worker will be relieved of all the tiresome, routine tasks by computerisation so that he or she will be concerned almost entirely with qualitative value judgements. This will enormously enhance the creativity of those involved and permit them to give full vent to their originality. We are led to believe that the judgements they reach will be consistent. We will think their judgements are logical and scientific because they will be based on mathematical models, and as we all know, or will soon be induced to believe, mathematical models are absolutely objective. The knowledge worker will, therefore, be able to make judgements in the interest of the whole community or class.

Subjective judgements, guesswork, hit and miss techniques and, in particular, the so-called 'common sense' and opinions of ordinary people will be superfluous. Or, their opinions may be more than superfluous, perhaps even disruptive and dangerous, if these people cannot understand the complex mathematical judgements on which these decisions are based. There will therefore be scientific ways of deciding what is good for us and, of course, we will be totally free to select from a range of pre-determined, logical alternatives. These alternatives will be good, not only for us, but for the large corporation and society in general. In fact we will be living, according to the scenario, in a sort of grandiose pluralism.

Because they will provide a rational basis for our society, these knowledge workers will behave in a rational manner at a personal, professional and social level. In these circumstances it would be quite inappropriate, and even unprofessional, of them to belong to partisan organisations such as trade unions, community pressure groups, or radical political parties. It would in any case, so this scenario suggests, be quite unnecessary for them to belong to trade unions because their knowledge and objectivity will be rewarded by good wages, fringe benefits which are denied to other workers, and they will have a watertight job security situation. But above all this, their work will be stimulating, because what could be more stimulating than the pursuit of knowledge and its application.

The knowledge worker will be cherished and respected by the community as he diligently applies his store of knowledge to improve not only his own quality of life, but that of the community at large. After all, if systems theory and technology can land human beings on the moon, it can most certainly solve our simple social problems.

One of the most powerful reasons that this scenario can hold any credibility at all is because each knowledge worker simply believes it is his fault as an individual that he did not make life good. He might feel that his qualification is not good enough; his experience not appropriate; or his attitude to life not dynamic enough to make use of the opportunities that are said to exist. Each individual is made to feel personally responsible for his plight, rather than recognising that it has been imposed on him by the social system, and that it is a plight which is shared by millions of other workers in the technologically advanced societies.

Summary

Workers are dehumanised by the degradation of the dole queue (or fear of it), dehumanised by Taylorism, dehumanised by being subordinated to a machine, or dehumanised by having their skills and ability taken from them as the misuse of science and technology reduces the actual qualification of more and more workers by hand and by brain (Braverman 1974). There are signs, however, that scientists and technologists are realising the crushing reality of this situation, and are attempting, as human beings always have throughout history, to gain control over the manner in which their own lives are lived (Elliott 1976). Although these developments are as yet embryonic, they do auger well for the future. Groups of workers by hand and brain are combining together and demanding that they have the right to produce not only socially useful products, but the right to produce them in an entirely different and more humane fashion (Lucas Combine, 1975).

The barriers to the humanisation of work are not technological. They are profoundly political and ideological. The humanisation of work cannot be achieved by any structural fiddling such as Group Technology, Job Enlargement, or Job Redesign. To be meaningful it must take into account the following:

1. The need for fundamental political change.
2. The need to change the ownership of the means of production.
3. To move towards a society which puts people first and profit and fixed capital second.
4. A recognition of the non-neutrality of our science and technology.
5. The development of a 'people centred' science and technology.
6. An examination of our machine and equipment design methodology and assumptions in light of 4 and 5 above.
7. The right of those who work in an organisation to design its main operational features democratically.
8. A reversal of the main features of work organisation introduced during the era of Taylorism.
9. The right to work for all those who are able and willing to do so.

References

Babbage, C., *On The Economy of Machinery and Manufactures* (Kelly, New York, 1832 (reprinted 1963)).

Bernholz, A., 'Proceedings: C.A.D. Conference. 'International Federation of Information Processing' (Eindhoven, The Netherlands, 1973).

Braverman, H., *Labor and Monopoly Capital – The Degradation of Work in the Twentieth Century* (Monthly Review Press, New York and London, 1974).

Cooley, M.J.E., *Computer Aided Design – Its Nature and Implications* (AUEW – TASS, Richmond, Surrey, 1972).

Cooley, M.J.E., 'Dialectics of the Man/Machine Interaction' in *The Open University Man-made Futures Work File* (The Open University Press, Milton Keynes, 1975).

Cooley, M.J.E., Proceedings: 'Gesellschaft Für Informatik, 1974' (Springer Verlag, Berlin, 1975).

Cooley, M.J.E., 'The University as a Factory', *New Scientist*, June 1976; 70 (1006).

——, 'Social Aspects of Computer Aided Design', in Proceedings: Computer Aided Design Conference, 1976. I.P.C. (Science and Technology Press, Guildford, 1976).

Dickson, D., *Alternative Technology and The Politics of Technical Change* (Fontana/Collins, London, 1974).

Elliott, D. & Elliot, R., *The Control of Technology* (Wykeham Publications, London, 1976).

Gomolak, L. and Raithel, H., 'The Bouncers Are Coming, *Financial Times* (22 February 1974) 19.

Gorz, A., 'The Tyranny of the Factory: To-day and Tomorrow', in A. Gorz (ed.), *The Division of Labour* (The Harvester Press Ltd, UK, 1976).

Hoos, I., 'When The Computer Takes Over The Office', *Harvard Business Review* (1960) 38, (4).

International Labour Office, 'Convention Number 120', Geneva.

Jungk, R., 'Politik und Technokratie', in *Aufgabe Zukunft-Qualität Des Lebens* (Europaische Verlagsanstalt, 1973).

Kling, R., 'Towards a People Centred Computer Technology', Proceedings: Association Computer Machinery National Conference, 1974.

Koeppe, E., *The Significance of Manware In the Design of Hospital Information Systems* (Freie Universität, Berlin, 1974).

Kornhauser, A., *Mental Health of the Industrial Worker* (John Miller Press New York, 1965).

Lucas Combine, *Corporate Plan*, (Lucas Aerospace Combined Shop Stewards Hayes, Middlesex, 1976).

Mott, P.E., *Shift Work, The Social, Psychological and Physical Consequences* (Ann Arbor, 1975).

Rose, S., 'Can Science Be Neutral?' Proceedings of the Royal Institute (45, 1972)

Rosenbrock, H., 'The Future of Control', UMIST/Report (University of Manchester Institute of Science and Technology, 1975).

Taylor, F.W., *Principles of Scientific Management* (Harper and Row, New York, 1947).

Zemanek, H., 'Human Choice And Computers' International Federation of Information Processing Proceedings (North-Holland Amsterdam 1975).

5 WORKER EDUCATION FOR INDUSTRIAL DEMOCRACY

W. Wilson and J.B. Nichol

Introduction

The creation of a workplace which gives meaning to work and contributes meaning to peoples' lives is a primary issue confronting modern technological societies. It is the conviction of the authors that this challenge can only be met by the full involvement of the working people, through the creation of an authentic industrial democracy.

Trade unionists and managers often seem to talk different languages when discussing industrial problems. The trade unionists speak a rhetoric more appropriate to the 1930s while the managers use an arid rationality seemingly out of touch with the lives of ordinary people. W. Wilson (1976) investigated workers' views (in the study which forms the basis of this paper). He presented to groups for discussion key terms such as: management, capital and nationalisation. Two dominant themes emerged: the workers did not trust management and they were sceptical of the commitment of their own union officials. For the workers the very word management had connotations of class, conniving and exploitation. Organisations in which such mistrust is prevalent, and where words have such different meaning, are fundamentally flawed. Under such conditions it is neither possible to develop the organisations' productive potential, nor job satisfaction for employees. In this paper we propose an educational approach which could restore trust and confidence in organisations.

The idea for this paper emerged out of conversations with Paulo Freire, a Brazilian educator, in Manchester in 1975. Freire has developed an effective method of education which has a potential application to worker education in Britain. He developed national programmes of adult literacy in both Brazil and Chile. The scope of his educational theories offer practical solutions to the problem of preparing workers for industrial democracy in Britain. Freire's method of adult literacy education aims at more than the development of reading and writing skills: it develops an awareness of the peasant's situation in society so that the peasant might act to transform his reality.

Freire came to Manchester to talk about development problems in

Worker Education for Industrial Democracy

Third World countries. In the discussions similarities emerged between the circumstances of the working man in British industry and the peasant in Brazilian society. Freire (1972) characterises the peasant as fatalistically resigned to the status quo: Argyris (1957) describes the modern working man's relationship to his organisation as passive, dependent and reactive. The peasant who is illiterate (the vast majority) have no vote: the working man has a very limited influence on the decisions which affect his working life.

In Brazil only those people who are literate has the right to vote. The success of Freire's method not only brought about literacy but won for many people the right to take part in the government of their country. Significantly his method is now banned by the ruling elite in Brazil and Paulo Freire now lives in exile. An effective educational programme for workers in Britain, through which they will assume a greater measure of control over their place of work, will be seen as a subversive activity by some people. We are convinced that the way to restore humanity to the work place is through a meaningful industrial democracy. To bring this about needs a massive programme of worker education so that the workers can act to transform their reality.

Paulo Freire is arguably the most influential theorist in the history of adult education. The T-group method is perhaps the most significant innovation in educational practice in this century. To us there is an important relationship between Freire's ideas and the T-group. The 'T' stands for training and is an abbreviation of the original 'Basic Skills Training Group' in human relations developed in 1947 (Bradford, Gibb and Benne, 1964). A T-group is a meeting of some 8-12 people, with an experienced trainer, concerned to learn more about themselves and the way people related in order to influence change within organisations and communities. To an outsider the trainer's behaviour will seem rather odd, differing as it does so radically from the traditional role of the teacher. The trainer is relatively passive, intervening in the discussion about as often as the other members of the group. When he does intervene he might encourage the members to observe and reflect on events within the group. Or he may suggest members share the feelings that they experience in reaction to events within the group. At other times he may offer interpretations of member behaviour from the perspective of a particular theory.

What he will rarely do is take up a traditional didactic role and lecture to the group. To the trainer the T-group is an experience in which he joins with the group members to explore human behaviour. The T-group is a reaction against the modern human condition in which one person's carefully maintained façade meets another's equally considered façade. A goal of the experience is authenticity in encountering each other so that each person might grow. The effectiveness of the T-group method rests on the assumption that through the person understanding the socio-psychological processes which influence his actions he can more deliberately choose how to act.

We are working towards a synthesis of Freire's educational model and that of the T-group.

Freire's methods were developed for an oppressed group in society. We argue below that the working class is an oppressed class. Although the more apparent features of oppression have been removed in the course of this century: lock-outs, tied housing, subsistence wages, other less visible aspects of oppression persist. They include alienation, unemployment, and authoritarian management ideologies. We will outline the principle features of Freire's philosophy and educational practice. The argument develops the analogy between the situation of the British worker and that of the Brazilian peasant. Then we explore the relationship between Freire's approach and the Western educational innovation, the T-group.

Our conclusion is that in Britain educators can develop in co-operation with workers an effective method of adult education. Such a method is an essential precursor to the emergence of a meaningful industrial democracy.

The sociological perspective

Society is created by men and in turn society creates the reality men experience (Berger 1966). Sociology and anthropology provide us with accounts of different societies: realities which are experienced by people with a certain absoluteness, and yet realities which are dependent for their very continuity on the acts of those people. There are societies in which the key features are radically different to our own British society. Religious beliefs, values attached to work, roles ascribed to men and women, systems of community leadership, rituals and taboos differ from one society to another. Comparative study illustrates the arbitrariness of aspects of our reality which we take as given and this suggests that we take a sceptical view of all aspects of our own society. A sceptical look at the practice of industrial life in Britain identifies a good number of dysfunctional beliefs, foremost of which is the belief in the inviolate right of a management elite to make the major decisions effecting working life.

The psychological perspective

A stream of psychological thought has developed (A. Maslow (1962), C. Rogers (1951), G. Kelly (1955)) which identifies and describes the potential for psychological growth that most human beings possess. This runs counter to the view (which pervades industrial life) that in adulthood personality is fixed. This does not mean denying other research into social systems which points to processes which *resist change* in men's roles, values and ideology. However, there is a vast difference between the position that the adult personality is inherently fixed and one in which personality does not change because of social mechanisms. To match those processes which hold back change are developments in educational methodology (Freire 1972, Bradford *et al.*, 1964) which *enable men to change themselves should they choose to do so*. These innovations in education offer working men the possibility of moving from a state of dependency to one of interdependency; to move out of resignation to become transformers of their reality.

The will to grow, which is in all men, the forces in society which repress men, and those forces within man himself which resist growth and change, form the basis of this paper.

Management Education in Britain

The culture of British industry has many magical beliefs. Some of these are as harmless as 'throwing salt over your shoulder'. Others are as destructive in human terms as the caste system. The predominant norms and beliefs in British managements, their concept of leadership and understanding of their workers and the learning process are destructive to the worker, the managers and the nation. These beliefs are part of the British social construction of industrial reality.

As such they have been handed down from former periods in our history. A century ago, when management and workers were relatively uneducated, simplistic notions of authority and work organisation were perhaps functionally appropriate. The work force today is highly educated and the inherited attitudes of management are now repressing an enormous productive capacity.

In the last few decades a management education programme has been implemented to release British management from outmoded assumptions about the nature of industrial man and his work. That the process for transformation must involve the workers as well has been realised more recently as evidenced by such organisation development strategies as job enrichment and autonomous work teams. We will argue in this paper that the focus of transformation should shift from being management-centred to being worker-centred. An aim of this paper is to prepare guide lines for such a radical shift in industrial education policy.

Industrial and the British class system

Britain is a society of class. Butler and Stokes (1969) found that the majority of people perceived themselves as associated with one of two classes, the middle class and the working class. When the relationship between class self-image and occupation was examined there was a strong correlation between managerial work and the middle class, and manual work and the working class.

Class stratification and its relationship to organisation hierarchies as a source of conflict in modern organisations is disputed. Darendorf (1963) is of the view that conflict is an inevitable accompaniment of social organisations and therefore industrial conflict does not necessarily have its basis in class. The emergence of the joint-stock company saw the separation of ownership control, and consequently defused the traditional Capital versus Labour conflict. Mills (1956) on the other hand, does not see that the separation of ownership and control has had a significant effect on class structure and control. He argues that owners and controllers, or stock-holders and managers, have such a similarity of outlook that they can be identified as a homogenous group.

MacRae (1975) pointed to a recent intensification of class feeling.

> What is true is that class fear, which is a kind of class consciousness has increased in the past three ot four years and is coupled to a shift in the class attitudes of the different generations so that those in their mid-twenties and early thirties manifest class feelings and hostility more appropriate to the 1840's than 1970's.

In a complex, changing industrial society there are a multitude of conflicting roles. The old simple class divisions become more complex: but there is sufficient evidence to support the theory of class conflict and suggest a hardening of class attitudes in recent years.

In modern industrial organisations control has been handed over to the professional manager by the owners, stock-holders or the state. *Those who control are the masters of those whom they control.* Herein is the first twist in the management-worker relationship.

The second twist is that a majority of managers see workers almost as a different type of man to themselves. McGregor (1960) noted that they assume workers dislike work, do not want responsibility and prefer to be told what to do. Consequently their function as managers is to coerce, control, direct and threaten subordinates. Of course implicit in their view of work organisation is that *they* have a capacity for self-direction and control, and responsibility and initiative. In other words, that in society we have two types of human beings — those who need to control and those who wish to be controlled; those who, if left on their own will act responsibly and those who will not. 'Don't worry yourself about them' said the manager of a company producing and installing ventilating systems, about to lay off a number of his erection team. 'They're not like us you know. If we were laid off it would be like the end of the world. But not for them. They don't mind, its part of their life.' (Wilson 1976).

The extent of the 'two beings' philosophy is borne out by the different treatment of managers and workers in industry. In many organisations canteen facilities for workers are separate from those for the managers. It is still possible to find the situation in which a father is controlled by the clock card and yet his graduate son, because of his higher organisational status, is not. Such 'apartheid' practices extend through into such things as methods of payment, shiftwork, promotion, sick pay leave, superannuation benefits and work content (Weddernburn 1970).

A further twist in the management-worker relationship is the attitude of one class to the other. Willmott and Young (1960) in their classic study of Woodford, a London suburb, provides some examples of middle class attitudes to the working class. 'The working class is wrongly named', said a company director, 'because they don't work at all judging by what happens in our firm.' 'I think the richest class today' said a works' manager, 'is the working class, and they don't know how to spend their money. They waste money on fridges, washing machines, T.V.s and cars.'

The problem in industry therefore is not simply one of different roles — those who manage and those who produce — but far more seriously the problem is one of different class. Coupled as this is with the antagonistic attitude of one class to the other where the culture, habits, likes, requirements of one are considered not simply *different* from but *superior*. It is precisely this division that Paulo Freire terms the oppressor/oppressed dichotomy.

The Thought and Method of Paulo Freire

On Oppression

Central to the thought of Paulo Freire (1972) is his belief that man's ontological vocation is to become more fully human. This humanity cannot be won for societies by those who oppress and exploit by virtue of their power, unless they are prepared to lose their power and identify with people. The task of liberation, of humanisation, must be the task of the oppressed: only their 'weakness' is sufficient to release not only the oppressed themselves, but also their oppressors. The oppressor who is himself dehumanised because he dehumanises others is unable to lead the struggle for a fuller humanity. Moreover the oppressed themselves are afraid of freedom, afraid to emerge from their domination and become responsible authentic beings in their own right. Having lived under the oppressor their consciousness has conformed to his prescriptions, they have internalised the image of the oppressor and adopted his guide lines. The central problem then becomes:

> How can the oppressed, as divided, unauthentic beings participate in developing the pedagogy of their liberation? Only as they discover themselves to be 'hosts' of the oppressor can they contribute to the midwifery of their liberating pedagogy. As long as they live in the duality where *to be* is *to be like* and *to be like* is *to be like the oppressor* this contribution is impossible. The pedagogy of the oppressed is an instrument for their critical discovery that both they and their oppressors are manifestations of dehumanisation. (Freire 1972, p. 25).

But this pedagogy is not idealism: according to Freire, oppression is a concrete situation, and consequently liberation must also be a concrete situation. The concrete situation of oppression must be transformed by praxis, reflection and action, into the concrete situation of freedom.

> If men produce social reality (which, in the inversion of the praxis turns back upon them and conditions them) then transforming that reality is an historical task, a task for men. (Freire 1972, p. 27).

And this task can only be fulfilled as men become conscious of their submergence in oppression, and turn upon it, and act to transform it. This is the process which Freire terms 'Conscientization'. 'Conscientization' means an awakening of consciousness, a change of mentality involving an accurate, realistic awareness of one's locus in nature and society; the capacity to analyse critically its causes and consequences, and rational action directed at transformation. (Sanders, T.G. 1968).

At some point in the historical process of these societies new facts occur which provoke the first attempt at self-awareness, whereupon a new cultural climate begins to form. Some previously alienated intellectual groups begin to integrate themselves with their cultural reality. Entering the world they perceive the old themes anew and grasp the tasks of their time. Bit by bit these groups begin to see themselves and their society from their own perspective; they become aware of their own potentialities. This is the point at which hopelessness begins to be replaced by hope. Thus nascent hope coincides with an increasingly critical perception of the concrete conditions of reality. (Freire 1974).

Freire distinguishes between three states of consciousness. The *semi-intransitive* consciousness of a people in a closed, totalitarian, society; their consciousness is circumscribed, either by some super reality — the prescription of reality by the elites, or magic and myth, or by a fatalistic acceptance of their own incapacity. Their consciousness is inactive: it does not cause them to act upon reality in order to change it. A *naive-transitive* consciousness arises when a society begins to open.

It is at this point in historical development that previously alienated intellectual groups, products of and belonging to the privileged elite, begin to identify and integrate themselves with the emerging oppressed. They thus intensify, by their critical consciousness of social reality, the drive for liberation, and through their communion with the people the *full transitive* consciousness develops.

Of course, during this transition the power elites, conscious themselves of the new consciousness and its challenge to their power, are anxious to maintain the status quo. Hence, they may first engage in superficial transformation, which gives the appearance of change, but which is designed to secure their position. Later, with the identification of the intellectual groups with the people, the growing challenge promotes the counter challenge of the *coup d'etat* and the recultivation by the coup of the 'culture of silence'.

On Technology

If the first attack on the fragile developing transitive popular consciousness is direct action by the power elites, the second is the much more subtle attack of 'technology'. There is an obvious dialectical relationship between technology and societies becoming more complex. But at a certain stage technology itself can dominate men's consciousness and reduce them to irrational myth-making. In short, technology becomes a 'species of new divinity'; evincing the worship of man. And it dehumanises in that it promotes 'specialisms'. The specialism shrinks the area of knowledge, and the specialist increasingly is unable to hold a vision of the whole, making reality unreal. And it dehumanises in that it de-problematizes. The people are directed by and prescribed for by technology. Every turn is indicated, every consequence presented.

P.L. Berger, B. Berger and Kellner (1973) elaborate how it is that technology influences man in their excellent analysis of modern consciousness in *The Homeless Mind*. They agree with Freire that the social institution of productive technology has a powerful effect on the way men construe reality influencing their very thought language with words from the world of machines. Whereas Freire indites the elites for the destructive effect of technology on men's humanness, Berger *et al.*, see it as an intrinsic consequence of technology separate from ideology.

On Education

In the thinking of Paulo Freire there can be no such thing as neutral education; education is either for domestication or for freedom. The method used in education for domestication he terms the 'banking method', whereas the method used in education for freedom he terms the 'problem posing' method.

In the banking method, which is the method used by the power elites, there is a dichotomy between students and teachers, and the students are treated as receptacles to be filled by the teachers. The attitudes and practices of the method are:

1. The teacher teaches and the students are taught.
2. The teacher disciplines and the students are disciplined.
3. The teacher chooses and enforces his choice, and the students comply.
4. The teacher acts and the students have the illusion of acting through the action of the teacher.
5. The teacher chooses the programme content and the students (who were not consulted) adapt to it.
6. The teacher confuses the authority of knowledge with his own professional authority, which he sets in opposition to the freedom of the students.
7. The teacher is the subject of the learning process, while the pupils are mere objects.

He concludes that is not surprising that the banking concept of education regards men as adaptable, manageable beings; therefore, the oppressive society uses this method to prevent the development of critical consciousness which would otherwise result from the students intervention in the world as transformers of that world. It is necessary for the oppressors, if they are to continue in their repression, to cultivate adaptability to, and therefore ready acceptance of, the 'given' situation.

The concept of education in the problem-posing method is the opposite of the banking concept:

1. The Teacher/student relationship becomes the teacher-student/student-teacher relationship.
2. The assumed false dichotomy between man and the world gives way to a knowledge of reality as the subject of man's consciousness, a reality which can be reflected upon and acted upon and thus transformed.
3. Liberating education is problem-posing education, it consists in acts of cognition, not the transference of information.

In problem-posing education men develop their power to perceive critically *the way they* exist in the world *with which* and *in which* they find themselves, they come to see the world not as a static reality, but as a reality in process, in transformation. (Freire 1972, p. 56).

4. It is dialogical not authoritarian, it consists of co-investigation and entails constant reconsideration.
5. Problem-posing education sets itself the task of demythologising reality, of unveiling it, and overcoming its false perceptions.
6. And problem-posing education is ongoing:

The unfinished character of men and the transformational character of reality necessitate that education be an ongoing activity. (Freire 1972, p. 57).

The problem-posing method through which Freire implements his philosophy is a critical, active, process through which habits of dependency are overcome. Teacher and student work towards a common goal, seeking truth about relevant problems. Both participate in a group trying to understand existence in a changing society. Through dialogue about meaningful situations in their life their awareness of their situation in society grows.

The stimulus to 'conscientization' derives from encounters in which one discovers the meaning of humanity. An almost inevitable consequence of the problem-posing method is political participation.

The traditional teacher/student dichotomy is radically altered: each teacher is also a student and each student a teacher. The object of action is the reality to be transformed — not the people. The transformation can only be carried out when the people themselves perceive their own situation and act upon it. The role of the co-ordinator (Freire uses this term in preference to teacher) is then to re-present to the people in an organised and systematised way the things about which they want to know more.

> [He will] come to know, through dialogue with the people, both the objective situation and their awareness of that situation — the various levels of perception of themselves and the world in which and with which they exist. (Freire 1972, p. 68).

The process begins with the present existential, concrete situation. The co-ordinator works *with* the people and not *for* them. His commitment to the people is total: in a very real way he must 'die' to the values and ways of his oppressor heritage in order to be 'reborn' through and with the oppressed. He does not believe in the myth of the ignorance of the people, but believes that in their development of critical consciousness and their transforming actions upon the world, they are moving towards the fulfilment of their humanity.

Man is constrained by the way he construes the world: the objective reality does not in itself limit the ways in which it is feasible for man to organise his society. Men must overcome their constructs of reality which limit them. Freire contends that the programme content of education should focus on 'limit situations' and help men recognise that beyond these there is an untested feasibility. Limit situations are located within a 'thematic universe' — which is a complex of interacting themes characteristic of a particular 'epoch'.

> An epoch is characterised by a complex of ideas, concepts, hopes, doubts, values, and challenges in dialectical interaction with their opposites, striving towards fulfilment. (Frèire 1972, p. 73).

The programme of education starts with an investigation of these generative themes, of the thematic universe of the people. The educator collects data on:

(a) the thought-language men use to refer to reality,
(b) the levels at which they perceive that reality,
(c) their view of the world, which is the source of their generative themes.

In Freire's literacy programmes the next step is the codification of the themes: this usually involves the use of photographs or sketches depicting real scenes or themes. The decoding of the material takes place within small 'culture circles'. Here the peasants react to the photographs or sketches, telling the group what they perceive in them; from this the co-ordinators re-present to the peasants their own reality as problems to be solved and acted upon. It is only at this stage that the problems of reading and writing are introduced. Literacy is now seen by the peasants to be a necessary element in their liberation: with it *they* can name the world, and thus act upon it and transform it. Accordingly the words used to develop literacy are the key words from their thematic universe.

In South America where Freire developed his educational method the pressing educational task was adult literacy. His primary goal was 'conscientization'. Adult literacy programmes became the vehicle through which the Brazilian peasant embarked on the process of discovering his humanity.

In Britain the pressing educational task is the working man's *organisational illiteracy*. For only through a developed awareness of the process of co-operative enterprise can he act to restore humanity to the world of work. Education for worker democracy in our society is the vehicle through which the goal of 'full-transitive consciousness' is to be achieved.

Freire and industrial society

The so-called First World has within it and against it its own Third World. And the Third World has its First World ... The Third World is in the last analysis, the world of silence, of oppression, of dependence, of exploitation, of the violence exercised by the ruling classes on the oppressed. (Freire 1973).

Lack of consciousness of oppression is a characteristic of oppressed groups and unjust social structures depend on this state of mind for their continuation.

Oppression in industrial society becomes visible when the oppressed group becomes aware and begins the process of liberation. We are alerted to oppression in our own societies by the awakening of consciousness of women, so long oppressed through traditional attitudes to a woman's role; the black community in America who have been through a rigorous process of conscientization in the past decade; and poor communities in urban slums who have reacted effectively against decisions made by planners about where and how they should live their lives.

A good example of the dynamics of liberation is the woman's movement. Our society has acknowledged that its women are an oppressed group. The traditional conception of the husband role is destructive to a woman's humanity. The authoritarian British husband does not intentionally 'enslave' his wife but his actions of colluding with the prevailing social norms have that effect. The women's liberation movement is altering our consciousness in Britain with remarkable rapidity. This 'transformation of reality' illustrates the key features of the process of an oppressed group breaking out from the domination of its oppressors.

Only the oppressed can act to transform reality.

It was women, the oppressed, who have initiated the transformation in Britain. It is ironic that on a second occasion it is the women that must ween men from their dependency. Herein lies Freire's argument that only the oppressed, in their 'weakness' can liberate both themselves and their oppressors.

The transformation of reality

The dismantling of myths surrounding the women's role has opened the eyes of many women to new vistas of reality. It is not a marginal difference in consciousness to see the real possibilities of a self independent of the prescriptions of a husband.

The repressive ploys of the oppressor

There is no absolute logic which dictates to a woman that she fit the normative woman's role in our society. Indeed as men resist the determination of women the manipulativeness and selfishness of the arguments for maintaining the status quo become clear.

Conscientisation – an awakening of consciousness

Until women began to articulate their grievances a majority lived unaware of the oppressive nature of the man/woman relationship in our society. People in an oppressor/oppressed relationship are not aware of their state. As consciousness grows the nature of the oppression is gradually illuminated. It is with amazement that we look back on how we were once.

In our society we are coming to understand the oppressive nature of sex roles. A further step towards a liberated society is the recognition of the oppression in the management/worker relationship. To label management as oppressors is to recognise the grave effect the relationship between manager and worker has on both parties' humanity.

Managers and workers in Britain today are still divided on the basis of class: the workers perceive in management's attitudes towards them a difference not simply related to the nature of work but to the nature of being: workers are different 'beings' to 'managers'. Of course this view is quickly contested by most managers who argue that in their relation to the means of production they stand in the same position as the workers. And on this basis they preach classlessness and harmony between managers and workers. But to the workers all the differential elements of class are still present — education, income, security of work, nature of work, prerequisites of work and (extensive consultative machinery not withstanding) control of work, and an expected differential attitude from those of 'lower order'. Of course it is quite logical for those of privilege to exhort everyone to work together, for only in this way can their privilege be preserved. But classlessness is a myth, and must be exposed as such, it must not be used to maintain the privileged position of a small minority.

Yet if industrial democracy means anything it must mean the right of workers — all workers, to control their own destiny, to create their *own* world. Any system which does not provide for this system is dehumanising.

A steward remarked in discussing management's redundancy plans during the 1975 recession: 'We don't have enough say in these matters. Yet it's *our* life in the future that's at stake' (Wilson 1976). And another remarked,

> Why should we just sit back when our futures, and that means the future of our wives and families, are being tossed about like confetti? All they seem to think we are is figures on a balance sheet. (Wilson 1976).

To restore the workers to humanity means 'freeing' them in the work situation: accepting their right to make their own reality. But this right can never be given by those who now control it, for that would involve a voluntary loss of their control, a control which they believe is theirs 'by right', or which they 'have earned', or is 'justified'.

Only the British worker can bring about their own humanisation: industrial democracy must grow from the developed critical consciousness of the workers.

Using Freire's three states of developing consciousness, the British industrial worker has on the whole moved beyond the semi-intransitive state. Although not under the total domination of the elites, he does not have the confidence of freedom required for full-transitive consciousness. He does not yet believe in himself. He cannot yet trust in his own perceptions and analysis. And he will not trust himself without a conscious educational effort. Before we examine what form such a programme might take, it is important to recognise what forces maintain the British worker in a naive-transitive state of consciousness.

The old myths of 'goals' and 'God', 'nature' and 'fate' have been replaced by the new myths of science and knowledge, technology and systems, capitalism and freedom, communism and oppression. The elites encourage belief in these new myths. They teach that the laws of science are absolute and inevitable and worthy of unquestioning obedience, and that knowledge, the sort which results from years of intense study and which therefore is open only to the minority, is a supreme virtue.

The elite believe that technology must be allowed to advance — even though it makes redundant hard won craftskills. Coupled with these myths is the belief that individual freedom can only be maintained by capitalism, that only a society that encourages people to 'use their initiative', to 'stand on their own two feet', can prosper and advance.

There are workers in our society who believe in such myths, people in whom the powerful persuasive propaganda finds a sympathetic response from 'the oppressor still housed within' (Freire 1972). But the majority of workers do not believe, but as yet are without the confidence to stamp their mind upon reality.

Elites prevent the development of full-critical consciousness within people through the retention of traditional teaching methods. The 'banking' method, education for domestication, is dominant in Britain. Teachers deliver knowledge. Whereas an education for freedom requires the exploration of the workers reality through dialogue in a problem-posing way. In industry emphasis is placed on job descriptions as the basis of training programmes. These descriptions are highly definitive and answer the question, What? rather than Why? The philosophy of 'train them in what they need to know to do their job' is carried over into management education and education of the workplace representative. And this attitude is not confined to management. The emphasis of the TUC in its Basic Training Course for Representatives is very definitely training. (The TUC is currently coming to broaden its general educational base with the launching of their multi-media scheme.)

Workers must not be trained too highly, they must not be taught to critically examine their social, economic, political or historical situation.

In these two ways the propagation of new myths and the retention of traditional teaching methods, the elite attempt to prevent the development of full critical consciousness within the British working man. But the pressures are there. Spontaneous action groups have arisen over the last ten years, and the pace of their emergence is quickening.

It is at this point that superficial transformation are enacted. Conscious of the mounting pressure for self-determination the elites of society and industry embark on 'ambitious' schemes of participation, consultation, and representation. The CBI, the TUC, the Government and the EEC have each produced their documents on industrial democracy, and two giant motor companies, Chrysler Corporation and British Leyland, have offered worker-participation schemes to their employees. But one must question this hastily developed enthusiasm for worker-participation.

> In industrialised countries, participation, particularly descending participation may be introduced by management in an attempt to attract and hold labour (particularly younger workers) and to cope with problems of absenteeism, spoilage, etc. Participation may also spread as a response to the need for the acceptance of technological change and changes in the structure of industry. A further factor is that in industries using advanced technology certain groups of key workers obtain such power that their participation in management has to be accepted by managers. (Walker 1973).

An examination of the suggested schemes for industrial democracy indicates that they will in no way affect the power structure within an industrial enterprise. The schemes most favoured by managements are those embracing consultation as the key element of democratisation (CBI 1973). But no matter how many levels of consultation are included, the ultimate 'right of management to manage' remains inviolate. Consultation — at whatever level — is not decision-taking. And if a man is deprived of the right to take decisions on matters relating to his being and his environment, that man is not free. He is under domination.

Workers are being offered only a superficial transformation, providing only the semblance of self-determination.

Herein lies the true role of industrial education: the awakening of consciousness in the industrial worker to the givenness of industrial life, and the development of critical consciousness enabling men to act creatively on their world.

The T-group

The affinity of the T-group method to Paulo Freire's approach struck us as remarkable. Freire does not refer to the T-group or other experiential learning groups which have emerged in America, nor to those writers who have described the method. This is surprising in view of the common origins. Both Freire's writings and the T-group are related through Buber, Sartre, Husserl, Fromm and Marcuse.

In 1946 Kurt Lewin and others developed an educational method which incorporated the values of democracy, science and the help-sharing relationship (Bradford, Gibb, Benne 1964). In the aftermath of World War II they were alarmed with the apparent threat to such values in the world. They noted the self-perpetuating character of social processes built on authoritarianism, competitiveness and elitism. To them such processes were destructive to humanness and indeed to the ideals of a democratic society. A solution was the replacement of such social processes with those which embodied life-enhancing values.

The development of an educational process in which such values were implicit seemed possible. This process would also be self-perpetuating and perhaps over time would displace educational systems based on authority and competition.

Concepts of a fixed cultural environment and of plastic learners who need to acquire skills and knowledge to live adequately in that environment run through much of traditional schooling. This group of social scientists rejected such concepts in favour of a model in which there is a reciprocal relationship between people and their society. People create social reality and in turn this social reality feeds back and creates the people. Reciprocity is a central feature of the T-group trainer's relationship to the group members; indeed it is reflected in the attempts to find a more appropriate term than trainer i.e. facilitator, staff member, resource person.

In Freire's method learning occurs within small groups called 'circles of culture'. He discusses the difference from traditional education in the relationship of 'teacher' to 'student' in such groups. He emphasises the extent to which the 'teacher' must merge with the people. The term he chooses for this person is co-ordinator.

The similarities between the two methods continue into practice. In the T-group participants discover that it is most productive to attend to processes in the 'here and now' rather than the 'there and then'. When learning about the self in relationships with others it makes sense to use the concrete experience of relationships within the group as the main vehicle for this learning. It is only a few steps beyond this realisation for the participant to discover the potential of the two person encounter. The sharing of each other's experience of existing as a human being, in openness and with trust, in an authentic way, is rich in meaningful learning. Such encounters are a characteristic of the effective T-group: two people meeting each other without the usual carefully maintained presentation of the self.

To be human is to experience existing in time and space at several levels simultaneously. Life is experienced at the level of our senses, our thoughts and our emotions. Within each of these there are further categories and levels. Traditional education emphasises the mind and, in particular, memorising facts. The T-group confronts the participant with the need for a reintegration of the levels at which reality is experienced.

These characteristics of the T-group method, the emphasis on the 'here and now', the centralness of the two person encounter and acknowledging a multi-level existence have their parallels in Freire's pedagogy. For him it is through the encounter with another that people discover the meaning of humanity. In a literacy group the curriculum grows out of the peasants' existential situation.

There are two primary goals in Freire's 'cultural circles', the manifest one of helping adults to learn to read and write and the meta-goal of 'conscientization', raising the level of consciousness of the adult to his situation in the world. The innovators of the T-group initially developed their method to train 'change-agents'. By change-agent they meant those people who acted in society to facilitate the process of change. The term included such professional groups as educators, managers, social workers and therapists. Quite explicitly the objectives of the learning experience were to develop the participants' awareness of process at the levels of intra-person, the group, and the inter-group. The similarity of these objectives to the Freire concept of 'conscientization' is altogether marked. The participants in a T-group do not learn to read and write but they do learn as Freire would express it, to 'name their world' so that they might act to transform their reality.

The process of the T-group is, like the cultural circle, collaborative. The members work together with the trainer at understanding their existential situation. The trainer has no syllabus or other prescriptions. He offers himself as a resource to the group members and will work with them on the group's problems. The issues the group chooses to work on are those chosen by a consensual process. The trainer does not, as in the 'banking' concept of education, decide the content of the discussion. What the group chooses to focus on is unique to that group and the choice is a group decision.

Freire is less helpful to the co-ordinator in understanding group behaviour. His concepts of 'the oppressor within' and the co-ordinator's required 'humility' suggest that the learning process in the group might be problematic. Defensive behaviour (from leader or participant) in all its manifestations, denial, aggression, regression etc. appears not to exist. Freire only hints that groups in Brazil might go through the growth pains that a British adult educator is all too familiar with.

The strength of Freire's analysis is that it enables us to relate repressive *social processes* to individual growth. He is less helpful to us when he writes about those internal forces which block growth within the individual, in his terms 'the oppressor housed within'. T-group theory on the other hand provides insight into *the psychology of personal growth*. It enables the individual to understand why and how he might resist a change in his self-conception even though the altered perception is an enhanced view of the self. Freire writes of the peasant giving up his fatalistic resignation to his life situation for a politically active role in society. In this paper we argue for enabling the worker to move from a state of reactive dependency to pro-active interdependency. Let us be clear that both prescriptions involve a radical change in self-conception and will inevitably encounter psychological resistance. The self-knowledge that the T-group can yield us, as in instances such as these, to override our defensive resistance to change when we chose to do so. Thus, the two bodies of theory are essentially complementary, Freire's sociological perspective lending strength to the psychological orientation of the T-group writers.

Experience in Britain

Both methods, Freire's and the T-group, were developed outside Britain. We have practised both and believe that with sensitive adjustment they offer solutions to problems within this society. A recurring issue that has emerged in using the methods is the extent to which the British adult has been 'put down' during his life. Practices of parenthood, authoritarian schools, the emphasis on streaming and examinations within the educational system, and the repression of emotional expressiveness in British society work in a co-ordinated way such that it is a fortunate person who emerges in adult life with a robust feeling of self-worth. Our work with T-groups suggests that the development of a group climate of unwavering affirmation for each member is the trainer's first task. Under these conditions group members begin to realise their potential to become creative, zestful, and caring people. This issue of self-worth or lack of confidence emerged in a study of shop stewards by W. Wilson (1976). In his research he applied Freire's notion of a social group's thematic universe. He investigated the trade unionists' perception of industrial life, that is the way they construed the reality of work. Three dominant themes emerged in the lives of industrial workers:

1. Distrust of management.
2. Scepticism concerning the commitment of their full-time union officials.
3. Lack of confidence in themselves.

Why should workers trust authority when through their lives people in authority have tended to exploit their weakness and diminish their worth as human beings? Their lack of confidence ties in with the lack of self-regard which emerges as an issue in T-groups.

Wilson's data suggests that a task of the educator with British workers is to redress the years of invalidation.

In the same work Wilson presents a tentative word code in which the thought language of the workers is explored. A part of this code is presented in Table I. Group discussions were held with shop stewards and these were tape-recorded. The recordings were analysed for the meaning associated with various key words, which he calls the initial perception. The developed dimensions represent the meaning that the educator or co-ordinator may use to problematise group discussions.

The word code was developed from informal discussions with trade unionists. Quite apparently there is a difference between the meaning a manager might associate with a word and that of this group. Differences of this kind will distort communication between managers and workers. The associations of meaning presented in the word code look hackneyed and prejudiced. Nevertheless we have demonstrated in this paper that

Table I: Word-Code and Analysis of Shop Stewards Thought Language

Word	Initial Perceptions	Developed Dimensions
Arbitration	Scepticism about impartiality of the arbitrators. Too far removed from the workplace. In hands of 'professionals'.	Value of 'objectivity'. Feasibility of impartiality. The 'rights' of arbitration panel. Effectiveness of decisions made.
Bureaucracy	Creating unnecessary jobs. Empire building. Complicating simple issues.	Problems of organisation and control. Efficiency. Size.
Capitalism	Exploitation. Bosses. Control by the rich. Selfishness. Unearned wealth.	Sources of money. Role of labour. Control of prices, wages. Competition. Export/Import. World markets.
Management	Conniving. Devious. Class, status. Paid to do a job.	The conflicts of roles in industrial organisations. The need for differentiation/integration of activities. Separation of ownership and control.
Nationalisation	More bureaucracy. Proliferation of staff jobs. Buck passing. Too many levels of decision taking.	Different forms of ownership of means of production. Relationship between ownership and control.

Source: W. Wilson (1976).

there is a reality in such negative connotations of 'capital and 'manager'. Those concerned with worker education need to heed these elements of meaning in such key words. A co-ordinator working with groups of workers needs to know the reality presented in this language. The co-ordinator's goal is to develop a set of words together with the workers, with which the problems of organisational life can be 'rationally' discussed and with which 'rational' action can be taken. By rationality we mean that which makes sense to the workers and not the prescribed rationality of government economists, management or Marxists.

Conclusion

Freire's cultural circles and T-groups have evolved out of particular cultural backgrounds. The background to these two methods suggest that neither can be simply imported into our society. Educators together with workers need to evolve a methodology which is indigenous to the British industrial culture. However, this does not mean the Brazilian and American experience should be ignored, rather it needs to be creatively woven into the British praxis, action and reflection, of the worker educator.

Oppression is a fact in British Industry, a singularly important one of which education for industrial democracy must take account. Freire's methodology, founded on values which are antithetical to oppressive social systems, together with the insights of the T-group theorists offers a theoretical base for worker education. Such a radical educational development is an important precursor to an authentic system of industrial democracy in Britain.

References

Argyris, C., *Personality and Organisation* (Harper and Row, 1957).
Berger, P.L., *An Invitation to Sociology* (Penguin, 1966).
Berger, P.L., Berger, B. and Kellner, H., *The Homeless Mind* (Pelican, 1974).
Bradford, L.P.,Gibb J.R., Benne, K.D., *T-group Theory and Laboratory Method* (Wiley, 1964).
Butler, D. and Stokes, D., *Political Change in Britain* (Macmillan, 1969).
Confederation of British Industry, *A new look at the responsibilities of the British public company: an interim report for discussion*, January 1973 and *The Responsibilities of the British Public company*: Final Report of the Company Affairs Committee (October, 1973).
Daredorf, R., *Class and Class Conflicts in Industrial Societies* (Routledge and Kegan Paul, 1963).
Freire, P., *The Pedagogy of the Oppressed* (Penguin, 1972).
——, *Cultural Action for Freedom* (Penguin, 1972).
——, 'Education, Liberation and the Church, *Study Encounter* vol. ix No. 1 (World Council of Churches, 1973).
——, Education for Critical Consciousness, (Sheed and Ward, 1974)
Kelly, G., *The Psychology of Personal Constructs*, vols. 1 and 2 (Norton 1955).
MacRae, *Is Britain a Fair Society* Part 1, 'The Shift in Class Attitudes' (Daily Telegraph 19 1975).
McGregor, D., *The Human Side of Enterprise* (McGraw Hill, 1960).
Maslow, A.H., *Towards a Psychology of Being* (Van Nostrand, New York, 1962).
Mills, C.W., *The New Men of Power* (New York, 1954) and *The Power Elite* (Oxford University Press, 1956).
Rogers, C., *Client-centred Therapy* (Houghton Mifflin, Boston, 1951).
Sanders, T.G., *The Paulo Freire Method Literacy Training and Conscientization*, (American University Field Staff, 1968).
Walker, K.F., *Workers' Participation in Management. Problems, Practice and Prospects*, p. 31 (International Institute of Labour Studies: 12, 1973).
Weddernburn, D., 'Work Place Inequality', *New Society*, April 1970.

Willmott, P. and Young, M., *Family and Class in a London Suburb* (Routledge and Kegan Paul, 1960).
Wilson, W., 'Education for Worker-Participation in Industry, unpublished M.Ed. Thesis, (Department of Adult and Higher Education, The University of Manchester, 1976).

6 ALIENATION IN THE WORKPLACE: A TRANSACTIONAL ANALYSIS APPROACH

Mary Cox and Charles Cox

Introduction

During the first half of this century social scientists have made an increasing investment of time and energy in the search for understanding both the basic nature of Man himself, and, among other particular aspects, the nature of man and the way he works. Traditional studies focussed mainly on technical efficiency, and the concept of Man as a living, wanting, animal was submerged beneath a welter of data on job analysis and job efficiency. The swing away from this approach was marked by the discoveries made by Elton Mayo (1933) during his research at the Hawthorne Plant, of the Western Electric Company in the late 1920s, when it became clear that the positive response of workers was not due to varying environmental influences so much as to the recognition they were being given.

Since that time models and theories of motivation, of organisational change, and managerial styles, have proliferated, some to have more impact than others.

Running alongside these studies of human behaviour in the work situation has been the equally important development of theories and models to explain individual behaviour, particularly with a view to creating effective therapeutic techniques to facilitate growth and change. One of these, Transactional Analysis, created by Eric Berne (1964, 1963) twenty years ago and still actively being developed, has provided a basic framework for describing and understanding personality and behaviour in such a way that it can be used effectively both as a psychotherapy and, more recently, as a tool in management and organisational development.

Transactional Analysis (TA) is a set of related concepts which describe personality structure and its behavioural manifestation (Structural Analysis), the ways in which people relate to each other (Transactional Analysis proper), the ways in which people can avoid relating effectively and productively (Game Analysis) and how a person comes to have chosen his particular way of relating to himself, to other individuals, and to the world in general (Script Analysis).

In this chapter we intend to look at some of the basic concepts in TA and use the model to examine the concept of *alienation* as it is manifested in organisation settings. Alienation as we understand it is the feeling of isolation or unconnectedness, the lack of emotional and psychological involvement that individuals experience within their organisation. This feeling frequently leads to a withdrawal of active commitment to work and can account for counter-productive behaviours such as subversive action or strikes. It is most obviously seen and heard in the 'don't care if I do or I don't' attitude in employees and openly expressed in the form 'They don't care what happens to me, they never take any notice when I do do a good job, so what's the point of doing more than I have to.' The greatest loss to an organisation when employees at any level feel alienated is that of creative energy and willingness to initiate action. Employees may comply or rebel but either way are unwilling, or feel unable, to use their personal skill and resources to achieve organisational goals, and generally refuse to take any responsibility for outcomes of actions.

What follows is a summary of basic transactional analysis, sufficient we hope, to enable the reader to understand alienation as described in TA terms, since we believe that this approach offers some immediate options for alternative action.

Structural Analysis is based on a theory of 'ego states'. An ego state is a 'consistent pattern of feelings and experiences directly related to a corresponding consistent pattern of behaviour' (Ellis 1974). It is a way of *being*. Each person has three ego states, or groups of feelings, experiences and behaviours, namely, Parent ego state, Adult ego state, and Child ego state. For ease, when referring to an ego state, the name is capitalised to distinguish it from the normal use of the word.

The Child ego state is the collection of childhood experiences, feelings, reactions and decisions. When a baby is born, unless he is physiologically damaged, he is a reactive organism. He will respond with feelings and behaviour to events outside himself and to internal stimuli, such as hunger and discomfort, and his expression of himself is free and total. This is the Free or Natural part of the Child. Between eight and ten months, in healthy children, it is evident that cognitive processing is active, and the baby can figure out primitive casual relationships between himself and external events. He is, at this stage, working in a very intuitive way and this part of the Child, which is the beginning of the Adult ego state, is called in TA the 'Little Professor'. In addition, the child comes to recognise, through using his Little Professor, that some of his behaviours produce certain responses from

Alienation in the Workplace

those around him and he begins to adapt his natural behaviour in order to get the most favourable effect, or in order to avoid an unfavourable effect. This part is called the Adapted Child.

During the early years of his life, if he is to survive, the child must be cared for by others, and part of him is recording impressions and experiences of significant others. He is not only adapting to them but modelling from them, incorporating into himself their feelings, their views and attitudes, their behaviours. This is the basis for the formation of the Parent ego state. The Parent ego state is a recording of other's attitudes, feelings and ways of behaving; it is the source of positive and negative value judgements, of permissions and prohibitions. There are three basic functions of the Parent: *nurturing* (the active giving of care to promote healthy growth), *controlling* (the caring use of prohibition to protect and sustain health and growth), and *standard setting* (the provisions of limits and standards for guidance and support). Since the young child (before the age of ten) is not able to use rational thinking (Jean Piaget, 1926) the data and experiences are incorporated into the Parent without examination and re-assessment of Parent data is necessary from time to time in later life in order to update it and check for validity in present circumstances. (Hence, the value of Management Development programmes in organisations.)

This evaluation and selection on a criterion of 'appropriateness to the here and now situation' is the function of the Adult ego state. The Adult is characterised by rational cognitive processing. It is this part of a person that can process information and events in an objective way, can estimate probabilities and likely outcomes, and make decisions based both on present and past experience. The Adult can use both internal and external data, can assess the relevance of data, can hypothesise, and can model reality in abstract thinking.

We can diagram this way of looking at personality structure (see over).

Each person has available to him energy, and how he feels and behaves depends upon which ego state is energised or *cathected*. As a person grows he has, if his development is healthy, increasing charge over himself, since he can use his Adult to think about his own behaviour and the responses of others to him. He will have available to him all three parts of himself and will experience freedom of choice within appropriate limitations. However, for a variety of reasons, some of which will be described later under the heading 'script analysis', many of us do not experience ourselves as free, or as freely as we might. There may be data in the Parent which is prohibitive and outdated, or inaccurate, which will result in ineffective or even harmful adaptation of the Child.

Diagram 1: The Three Ego States

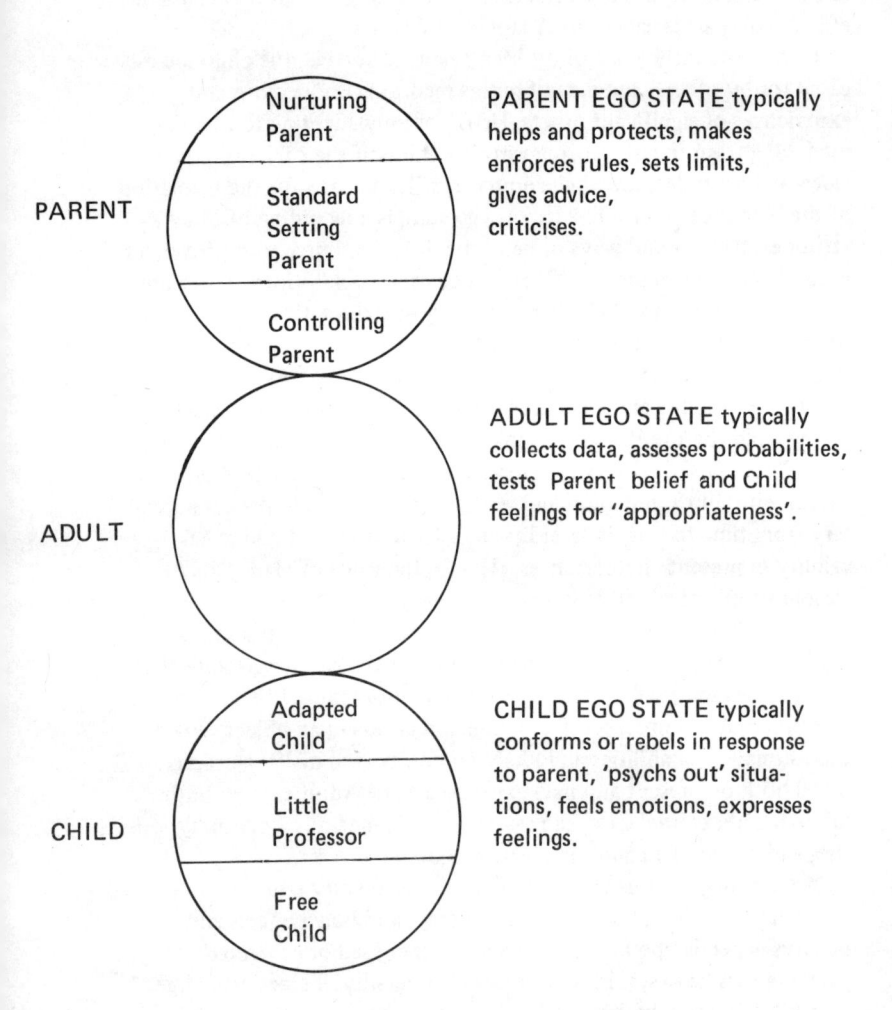

PARENT
- Nurturing Parent
- Standard Setting Parent
- Controlling Parent

PARENT EGO STATE typically helps and protects, makes enforces rules, sets limits, gives advice, criticises.

ADULT

ADULT EGO STATE typically collects data, assesses probabilities, tests Parent belief and Child feelings for "appropriateness".

CHILD
- Adapted Child
- Little Professor
- Free Child

CHILD EGO STATE typically conforms or rebels in response to parent, 'psychs out' situations, feels emotions, expresses feelings.

There may be present in the Child fears and fantasies which have not been properly examined by the Adult and rejected in the light of more favourable evidence.

Two phenomena are worth mentioning at this point, albeit briefly. It may happen that the boundaries between ego states are either lax or too rigid. In the first case, *contamination* occurs and Adult functioning is impaired by the interference of either Parent or Child, and sometimes by both. What is seen and heard from a person whose Adult is contaminated sounds and appears to be an Adult statement, but when checked out by someone else's uncontaminated Adult will be seen to be held in contradiction to here and now evidence from reality. Examples of this are prejudicial statements such as 'Women don't usually make good bosses over men' (Parent contamination), and 'You can't ask my boss for help with anything, he just gets angry' (Child contamination).

In the case of boundaries between ego states being too rigid, it is difficult for a person to cathect a particular ego state and *exclusion* occurs. Exclusion may be temporary or it may be a long term characteristic, for example, a person may generally exclude his Free Child, never allowing himself to feel or express himself naturally; or he may exclude his Parent because it is over-controlling, and act without conscience. Yet again, the Adult may be excluded, particularly if the person's Parent is heavily controlling and has forbidden the person, when young, to think for himself. It is possible for two ego states to be excluded, in which case, a person comes constantly from the remaining ego state; constant Child (always out for a laugh and a good time), constant Adult (always thinking and assessing, staying away from feelings), constant Parent (dogmatic, authoritarian and controlling).

Transactions

A *transaction* occurs when there is a stimulus from one ego state and a response from another ego state, either a different ego state within the same person, or any one of the three ego states in another person. Ellis (1974) defined transaction as 'a unit of social action in which each person gains something'. A series of transactions forms a conversation.

> Whenever an individual initiates a transaction (or responds to a stimulus from another person) he has a number of options as to which ego state he will use and to which ego state in the other person the stimulus will be directed. The healthy individual is autonomous in his choice of options and chooses to initiate or respond from the ego state he judges to be most useful in a given situation

(Woollams, Brown and Huige, 1974).

There are three kinds of transactions, parallel or complementary, crossed, and ulterior.

Diagram 2: Complementary Transactions

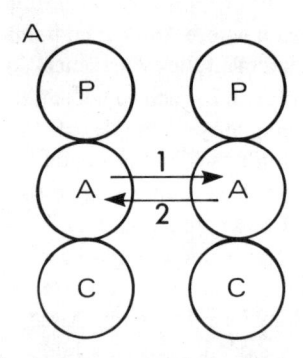

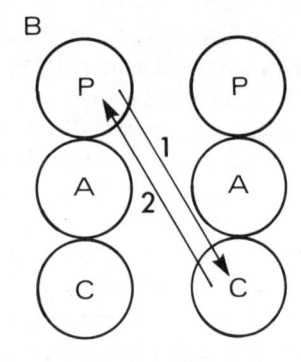

A

1. What time is it?
2. It's four o'clock

B

1. You look worried, can I help you?
2. Yes please, I really do not know how to do this.

In communication, as long as the transactions are parallel, the conversation may continue indefinitely.

Diagram 3: Crossed Transactions

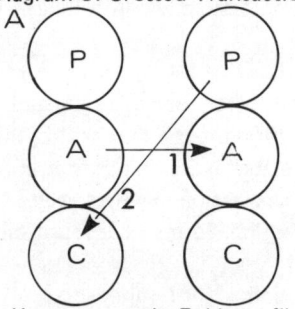

A

1. Have you seen the Robinson file?
2. If you put things away properly you would know where to find them!

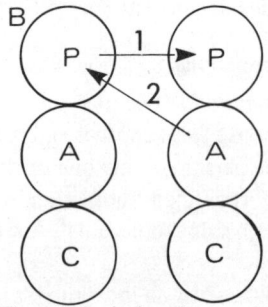

B

1. The standard of graduate trainees is just not what it was five years ago. They think they know it all — no respect for their superiors these days.
2. I have two very bright and helpful trainees this year.

Alienation in the Workplace

Crossing can occur in two ways, as shown. Both involve a response from a different ego state other than the one addressed. The effect of a cross-up is to stop the dialogue, even though this may be only for a few seconds. A more subtle cross-up can occur when a different part of the same ego state responds e.g. Free Child to Nuturing Parent is responded to by Critical or Controlling Parent to Adapted Child. It can be very useful to cross-up a transaction in order to shift a person from one ego state to another more appropriate one.

Diagram 4: Use of a Crossed Transaction to Cathect Adult

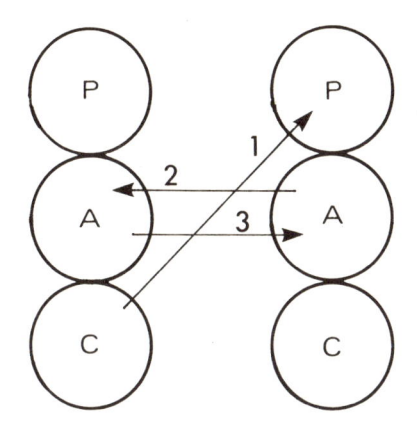

1. I really don't know what I am going to do. I am in such a mess. I will never get this report done on time.
2. You can take it home with you tonight and you still have five hours tomorrow.
3. Yes if I get organised I can just make it.

Ulterior transaction involve four ego states. There is an overt 'social' transaction (what is seen and heard out loud), and a covert, *psychological* transaction, which may or may not be experienced consciously by the persons involved. Wherever there is an ulterior, psychological transaction, it is this level to which attention will be paid, whether this is in awareness or not. It is not uncommon for people to report after a conversation that they were vaguely aware that 'something else was going on' during a dialogue.

Diagram 5: Ulterior Transactions

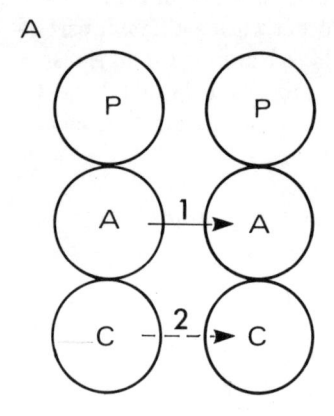

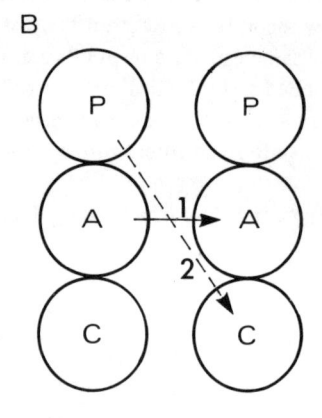

A

1. *Overt level* — I think we need to discuss this in more detail.
2. *Covert level* — I don't trust you.

B

1. *Overt level* — Did you check the data in these tables?
2. *Covert level* — You've messed it up again!

Stroking and time structuring

The ways in which we transact are closely related to our need to be stroked and the way in which we choose to structure our time. A stroke is a 'unit of recognition' (Ellis, 1974) and 'may be used as the fundamental unit of social action. An exchange of strokes constitutes a transaction, which is the unit of social intercourse' (Berne, 1964). When stroking takes place, a message is transmitted from one person to another which is intended to leave the receiver either comfortable and feeling good about himself (stroking is positive), or uncomfortable and feeling bad about himself (stroking is negative). One of the most simple examples of this is the use of the word *Hello*. To say hello to someone is to give them recognition, and it can be done in a variety of ways, some of which convey pleasure in seeking the person, others clearly indicating that the person's presence is undesirable. Saying 'Hello' is one of the simplest and most socially convenient ways we have of stroking each other, and most people can readily identify the feeling of having missed the stroke if someone we expect to recognise us does not say 'hello' to us.

One of the responsibilities, often intuitively recognised, of managers

Alienation in the Workplace

and supervisors, is to say 'Hello' (i.e. give daily strokes) to their subordinates. There are, however, many managers who do not consider this to be important, or actively condemn it as timewasting and 'soft'. (The writers have talked with managers who, after attending a TA program, have given more attention to this seemingly small issue and have been amazed and delighted at the effects of good daily stroking!)

Whilst a certain proportion of our daily transactions are Adult to Adult, usually aimed at getting some task worked through, a great many of our transactions are directed toward the giving and getting of strokes. The quantity and intensity of stroking required by each individual may be very different, but the need for strokes is as basic as the need for food, water and air. Each person varies in his choice of means for giving and receiving stroking. Strokes may be exchanged through open, straight transactions or through manipulation seen in ulterior transactions. A final, but important, issue is whether a person has developed the ability to give and receive positive strokes sufficient for his needs, or whether, through early and faulty decisions made by the Little Professor based on unhappy childhood experiences, he has decided to accept and give mainly negative strokes, believing that for him not enough positive strokes will be forthcoming.

Granted our basic need for recognition or stroking, how then do we set about meeting this need? As Berne so succinctly puts it, 'What do you say after you say 'Hello'?' (Berne, 1972). Berne proposes that each of us experiences 'structure-hunger'. That is, we have an existential need to fill the time between birth and death, between waking and sleeping, otherwise we are in danger of experiencing 'meaninglessness' which is psychologically and emotionally unacceptable. Each individual has choices open to him about how he will spend his time. What, then, are the gains to be had from each option?

There are, from a TA point of view, six ways of structuring time, each of them offering a particular way to transact, and to give and get strokes.

1. *Withdrawal*: when a person is withdrawn he is not engaging with another, though he may well be engaged in internal dialogue. Self stroking may occur either through remembering old strokes or through internal dialogue in which the Parent is stroking the Child.

2. *Ritual*: a stereotyped series of simple, complementary transactions, the aim of which is to give and get strokes. There may be variations in the words used but the basic structure of the exchanges is always

the same.

3. *Pastimes*: a series of semi-ritualistic transactions, the aim of which is to pass the time. Pastiming is seen in gossip and chit-chat, in situations where there is nothing else to do, or people wish to avoid doing what there is to be done.

4. *Activity*: the transactions are goal-oriented, aimed at producing something, and are mainly Adult to Adult, with opportunities for stroke exchanges from Parent to Child, or Child to Child.

5. *Games*: a game is a predictable set of transactions in which there is a social (overt) level, and a psychological (covert) level, ending with a pay-off (negative strokes), leaving one or both partners feeling uncomfortable. Games are always outside of awareness. The characteristic effect when the pay-off (negative strokes) is delivered is the experiencing of bad feelings (rackets). Games provide more intense stroking than rituals or pastimes, but the stroking is always negative.

6. *Intimacy or Authentic Encounter*: transactionally this can be defined as all three ego states in one person being available to all three ego states in the other. Each person is separate and autonomous, and is able to relate appropriately and openly to the other. In such a relationship stroking is at its most powerful.

In terms of achieving greater organisational effectiveness, managers and subordinates alike might usefully consider how their time together is structured, and what their investment is in choosing one structure rather than another. Very often the choice is determined not by the work to be achieved, or the problems to be solved, but by the individual psychological and emotional needs of each person, particularly in terms of stroking. The way an individual chooses to get his need for strokes met will determine the way he chooses to spend his time. Each person has certain fantasies in his Child and beliefs in his Parent about the best way to handle this. In order to understand how these attitudes and assumptions are formed and maintained it is necessary to explore to some extent the personal history of the individual, particularly to trace patterns of behaviour back to early Child decisions. This is *Script Analysis*.

Scripts

A script is an unconscious life-span based on early decisions made by a person's Child. It is the basis for his choice of strategy and behaviour and, unless such decisions are reviewed and re-evaluated for their appropriateness and relevance in the here and now, it is likely that a person will be behaving inappropriately and possibly destructively, using old data instead of acting autonomously in response to present reality. (The reader is referred to *Scripts People Live* by Claude Steiner (1974) for a fuller account of this.)

The importance of having some insight into what a script is, and how it can dictate a person's living is only relevant here insofar as it is helpful to understand that people have made certain decisions early in life about how they are going to relate to others, particularly with a view to how they will get their stroke needs met. Those decisions are likely to be inappropriate for handling present relationships, and may be either non-productive or actively counter-productive, as seen in the choice to play games rather than take the risk of relating openly. For example, a person may be raised with the message from his family, usually his parents, 'He who asks doesn't get'. The Child in the young person hears and understands this quite literally and decides that if he wants something, including personal recognition, he must find some way of getting it without directly asking for it. This will require some considerable strategy on the part of his Little Professor, especially if he is given the additional bind message 'And he who doesn't ask doesn't want.' That is to say, he will have to make his demands known through manipulative ulterior transactions.

Another fairly typical message in British culture is 'Don't get close' (emotionally). This may be either a blanket injunction or relate to specific types of relationship (i.e. to people of your own sex). How is a person who accepts this message to get his need for good strong stroking met? And, conversely, how can he give strong positive stroking to another, without getting close? Many people resolve this dilemma by simply deciding it is 'inappropriate' to give and get such stroking in the work situation, that it must be reserved for a few special relationships.

Curiously enough, the relationship between managers and subordinates, and often between peers, is frequently rather like a marriage relationship. Partners often choose each other because their scripts are complementary, and whilst they relate part of the time productively and straightforwardly to meet their own and each others needs, part of their relationship is characterised by manipulative, 'gamey' behaviour in the belief that this is the only option open to them to get certain personal needs met. When the strategies fail, either because of a lack of complementariness, or because the counter-productive side-effects outweigh the pay-offs sought, the danger is that the person will give up working to get his needs met within the relationship and the result is alienation. When explained in TA terms, we see alienation as the result of *stroke deprivation*, and suggest that those organisations in which alienation is a characteristic feature have an unhealthy stroke economy.

The underlying cause of an unhealthy stroke economy is to be found in the nature of the relationships and the resulting patterns of transactions, i.e. the way time is structured. The following is an example of what might occur between a manager and his subordinate. Mr A is a man who has accepted (in his Child) messages such as 'Be Strong — don't show your feelings'; and 'Men who show warmth and affection to other men are "sissy" — don't get close to your own sex.' He is, in fact, pleased with and proud of his young subordinate who he trained in his own department and who is ready to take on more responsibility. However, Mr A is unwilling to go against his own Parent and therefore does not let his subordinate know his feelings and evaluation. He tends, fairly typically, to work on the basis 'when you do something wrong I'll let you know; until then just carry on'. He is reticent in giving feedback and very grudging with his praise, probably critical with the good intention of giving the subordinate high standards to work to.

The subordinate will probably respond positively to what he at first interprets as the amount of freedom and responsibility he is granted. But he becomes dispirited (disappointed, frustrated Child) as he gradually realises that no matter how good the results he achieves Mr A will not come out with direct praise, much less any remark conveying personal pleasure and affection. It is not surprising then that the subordinate begins to feel there is no point in making special efforts, there is no pay-off for creative use of initiative. He feels unappreciated and his standard of work drops. He is sometimes late into the office, never stays on to finish something but leaves it until the next day. His Child excitement and enthusiasm wanes and he may say 'what is the point — nobody cares that much'. Mr A may feel puzzled, even hurt, by the change in his valued subordinate. He becomes even more critical and in so doing alienates the subordinate even further. The subordinate in turn begins to think 'He doesn't trust me any more.' He becomes unwilling to initiate. He may either rebel at this point and channel his disappointment and frustration into angry behaviours based on a Child decision to give Mr A something he can 'really moan about' or he may withdraw, possibly literally by leaving the department or even the organisation. Or, he may adapt even harder, seeking to please Mr A's Critical Parent.

Alienation in the Workplace

In each case the energy is re-directed away from productive and creative work into strategies for getting strokes, if not from Mr A, then from sympathetic colleagues or from a new boss. That is, he increasingly structures his time by pastiming or playing games with peers or with Mr A. An otherwise effective manager has lost the support and creative energy of a valuable subordinate, largely because he did not meet that subordinate's natural healthy need for personal recognition and praise. Both retire to a hurt, angry, puzzled position and from there engage in gamey transactions that not only are a waste of valuable time and energy but escalate the alienation.

Symbiosis

Many writers on organisations (McGregor (1960), Blake and Mouton (1964) and Argyris (1962)) have pointed out that the behaviour of many managers is basically parental. For example, McGregor's Theory X assumptions stem entirely from the Parent of the manager. His transactions are addressed to the Adapted Child of the subordinate. This is likely to result in compliant or rebellious behaviour on the part of the subordinate, thereby confirming the assumptions of the manager. This is what McGregor refers to as a 'self-fulfilling prophesy'.

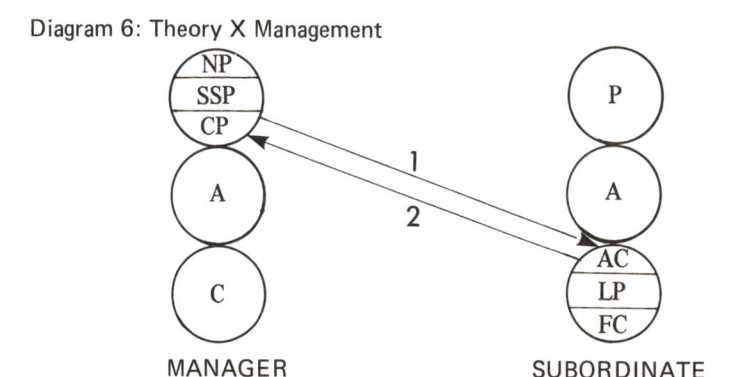

Diagram 6: Theory X Management

1. Manager relates from Controlling Parent to Adapted Child.
2. Subordinate responds from Adapted Child.

The subordinate can move away from this situation by responding from his Adult rather than his adapted Child, thus crossing the transaction. Alternatively, if the manager has his Adult available (for checking reality) as well as his Parent (for setting standards), and his Child (for creativity and fun), the subordinate will also be able to respond from any of all three ego states as appropriate. This is 'Theory Y' in operation.

Argyris (1962) has suggested that the traditional values in most organisations are such that management places a strong emphasis on setting objectives, believes that effectiveness increases as people are rational and decreases if people are emotional, and operates a mainly directive system of motivation by manipulating a range of rewards and punishments. This leads to a high level of judgemental feedback and associated defensiveness, which, in turn, produces conformity, mistrust and external commitment. In TA terms the manager is operating from Controlling Parent (judgemental feedback) and Adult (emphasis on rationality and objective setting). The subordinate is working from Adapted Child (defensiveness, mistrust and conformity).

Both Argyris and McGregor (Theory X) are describing *symbiosis* (Schiff 1975). This is a relationship in which one partner is primarily in Parent and Adult, with his Child excluded. The other is primarily in his Adapted Child, with Parent and Adult excluded. This is shown diagrammatically below:

Diagram 7: A Typical Symbiotic Relationship

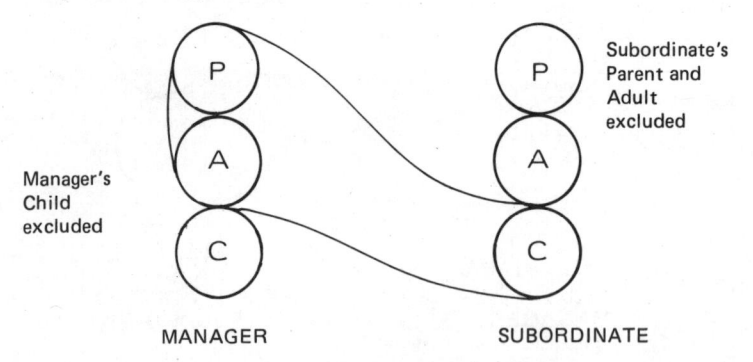

Such a relationship is characterised by dependency, since the subordinate partner has needs which he believes can only be met by the other. In effect, they together make up one total person rather than operating in relation to each other, but separately and autonomously. It is very common in organisations for 'symbiotic chains' to exist (as in diagram 8), with each level of management relating from Parent and

Alienation in the Workplace

Adult to the Child of their subordinates, but in turn relating to their superiors from Adapted Child.

Diagram 8: A Symbiotic Chain

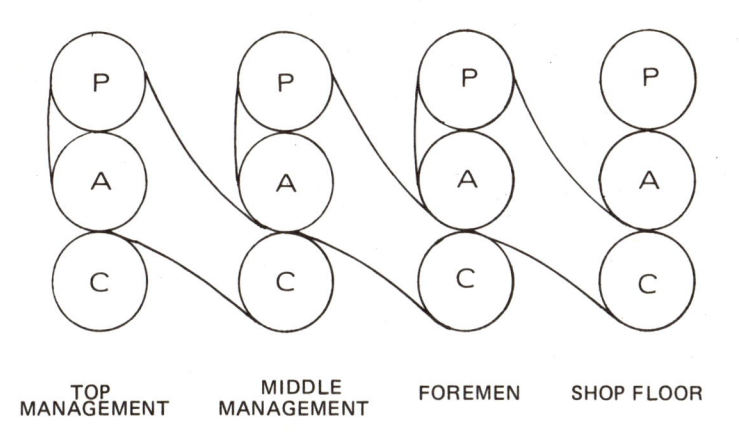

TOP MANAGEMENT   MIDDLE MANAGEMENT   FOREMEN   SHOP FLOOR

Another common occurrence is mutual symbiosis. This is as shown in diagram 9 and results in the partners being mutually dependent for satisfactory operation and fulfilment of their needs. This relationship of dependency, or in TA terms of symbiosis, is in our view, the key characteristic of an organisation in which alienation exists.

Diagram 9: Mutual Symbiosis

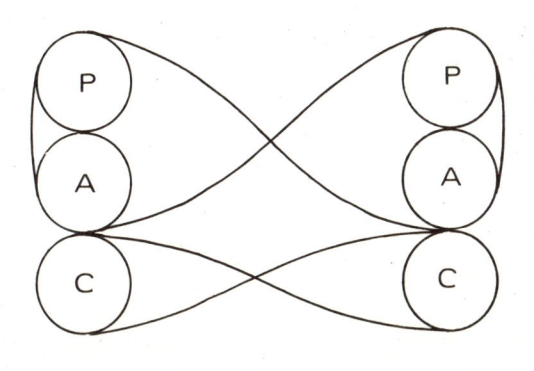

Each partner relates with his Parent and Adult to the Child of the other

One effect of a symbiotic relationship is that the dependent partner believes he can only get strokes by pleasing the other. The stroke supply is seen as limited, and conditional upon compliance. This is the direct result of the managerial values and behaviour described by Argyris and outlined above. An important characteristic of this situation is that individual growth is limited and productive adaptation to change is difficult. The one partner believes he cannot judge, think and decide effectively for himself, the other, that he is not permitted to take care of his own needs, but must always care for or control the other. In this state both partners are likely to experience frustration, feelings of inadequacy, and depression. This can be acute at the lower end of a symbiotic chain where the individual has no subordinates, and therefore spends his whole working life in the dependent position, rarely feeling even a limited ability to control his own destiny. At this stage the frustration is likely to escalate into a general feeling that 'there is nothing I can do', and productivity is replaced by *passivity* — a common complaint of bosses in relation to subordinates, and is in fact the situation classically described as alienation.

Passivity

Passivity is, then, the likely outcome of a symbiotic relationship or alienation, and is a state that is worth considering in some detail.

It always involves *discounting*, that is, the ignoring or minimising of some important and relevant aspect of the situation. Discounting involves either the exclusion or the contamination of the Adult. The external manifestations of this are *redefining* and *grandiosity*. 'Grandiosity is the purposeful exaggeration or minimisation of some characteristics of the self, other, or of situations' (Mellor & Schiff 1975). Illustrations of this are given by statements such as, 'You never like the work I do', or 'They're always fussing in the Production department, there's nothing really the matter.'

> Redefining refers to the mechanism people use to maintain their established view of themselves, other people and the world ... It is the means by which people defend themselves against stimuli which are inconsistent with their frames of reference ... (Mellor & Schiff 1975).

As with grandiosity, it involves discounting some aspect of the situation and is a protective mechanism, enabling the individual to avoid change, or taking responsibility for his actions. Redefining occurs when a

Alienation in the Workplace

person's response to another is connected with, but not logically related to, the original statement or question as, for example in the following interchange, illustrating both grandiosity and redefining on the part of the subordinate.

Boss: You have made three mistakes in this piece of work.
Subordinate: Nothing is the quality it used to be.

The effect of discounting in the situation of alienation is to enable the individual to avoid aspects of the situation which would conflict with his existing beliefs and frame of reference, and this enables him to continue with the passive behaviour. Since it involves the exclusion or contamination of the Adult the way to prevent it, is to cathect Adult. This can be done by crossing the transaction. One way to do this, is simply by a direct appeal to look at the available evidence.

It is worth noting in passing that there are styles of passive behaviour.

Namely:

1. *Simply doing nothing*: Often this stems from the feeling 'there is nothing I can do'. In extreme cases this can be accompanied by feelings of resentment and depression. In this case Child energy is being used to inhibit responses (passive resistance).

2. *Over-Adaptation*: This is extreme compliance. The person carries out whatever he is asked to do, often putting up an appearance of being anxious to please. This may be accompanied by great puzzlement as to what more could be expected. But the activity is characterised by lack of involvement and creativity. Energy is being used in compliance and subordinating self to authority. Rebelliousness springs from a similar psychological position. In this case energy is dissipated in unproductive counter-dependent behaviour.

3. *Agitation*: This is the use of energy in purposeless non-productive activities, e.g. excessive and irrelevant talking, pacing about, smoking.

4. *Incapacitation or Violence*: This is the last stand against change and the possible breaking of the symbiosis. The person simply becomes ill (gets ulcers, asthma, headaches, etc.) or loses his temper.

All the above behaviours may be seen in many organisation where symbiotic relationships exist. This has been well described by Wallgren (1975):

In organizations where the symbiotic relationship exists, the total organization is ineffective. In an effort to expand the direct span of control the top management makes and enforces rules in such a way as to reduce the ability of the individual member to accomplish in a stroke-producing manner. In an effort to maintain a more favorable stroke balance the members adapt passive behavior patterns. They do the minimum possible amount of work, i.e. they do nothing. They compliantly do only what they are ordered to do, i.e. they over adapt. They file grievances over meaningless issues, i.e. they agitate to avoid the real issues. They engage in one-down power plays which may include violent acts of organizational sabotage. The organizational impact of all forms of passivity is decreased effectiveness and increased frustration for all personnel.

A classic description of an alienated workplace.

The use of TA in reducing alienation

How then might transactional analysis be used to understand and overcome alienation? There are three stages in bringing about change. First there is *awareness*. For many people one of the good effects of understanding TA is that it sharpens the senses, and raises new perspectives which give a broader and deeper perception. Secondly, there is understanding of what is experienced. TA offers a model which is strongly diagnostic, and basically simple in both language and conception. Thirdly, there must be *willingness* to change. This last condition rests entirely with each individual, but, like McGregor (1960) and Maslow (1954), we believe that growth is a natural tendency, and that people are not only willing, but basically want to grow and be themselves as fully as possible. Very often what seems unwillingness to change, or to co-operate, is born of lack of belief that change is possible. For example, the Child in the person may be reacting to old Parent messages such as 'Don't ask questions, do as you're told'; 'You're OK as long as you please me — don't use your own initiative'; or 'Don't take risks.' To act against such Parent messages usually produces discomfort, anxiety, even fear, in the Child so that positive investment in experimentation and change is low.

One of the most powerful aspects of TA, we believe, is that it offers a 'world-view' in which each person is ultimately capable of taking charge of his own life, thinking his own thoughts, and feeling his own feelings; making his own decisions, and in so doing can remain

Alienation in the Workplace

caring and responsible. He can be himself, act autonomously, and relate healthily to others around him.

At this level some fundamental assumptions in TA are exposed, namely that there is a natural tendency in each person toward growth (self-actualisation) and the capacity or potential is present in each person to achieve this growth. Based on these assumptions (the most basic of which is 'I'm OK and You're OK') TA offers a framework for generating options, creating alternating strategies, for updating Parent data, decontaminating Adult functioning, and freeing Child energy and creativity. One of the effects of using a TA approach to problem solving, whether the problem is personal, interpersonal, or technical, is that an understanding of ego states produces useful insight not only into person to person communication (i.e. the nature of the transactions) but into internal conflict.

Once an individual can recognise his own internal 'voices' his conflict (for example between 'I want . . . but I ought . . .') is more readily understandable, in terms of Parent versus Child, and thus more readily resolved. This is done by engaging Adult which during conflict is usually excluded. It often is the case that Parent messages around getting Child needs met are restraining and sometimes prohibitive — e.g. 'Don't get close', 'Don't ask for what you want' 'Don't show your feelings,' 'Don't trust', 'Don't complain.' The individual experiences Child dissatisfaction but lacks Parent permission to do anything to deal with his discomfort. Typically he must either discount it, or hope that someone will notice and do something for him, or he will decide (with Little Professor) to 'get around' the Parent message by manipulative behaviour. 'I will get what I want but you won't know.' Yet another alternative is to get sick, have a minor accident, or engage in irritating behaviours (as seen in games such as 'Kick me', 'Stupid', 'Schliemiel' 'Wooden Leg' and 'Poor me' (Berne 1964)) on the basis of a decision to get needs met by being little and helpless (Adapted Child) or through negative stroking which is better than nothing. All of these manipulative behaviours are forms of passivity i.e. energy is being used to resist responsible involvement in goal oriented activity.

In terms of management and subordinates, or management and unions, for example, the passivity is negatively stroked thereby reinforcing it. Management's negative, and sometimes bitter, prophesies about lack of commitment and responsibility are fulfilled, opportunities for positive stroking are reduced and a vicious circle is set up — the stroke economy is unbalanced. Subordinates and/or unions become more and more dissatisfied and further and further alienated.

It seems to us that the first step in reducing alienation is to recognise and accept the need of each person for a healthy and adequate stroke diet. That is, both conditional and unconditional positive stroking must be available, so that the individual is stroked as much for being as for performance, and that the strokes be available from all three ego states, not just from Parent to Adapted Child.

It is a well-used saying in TA that 'You get what you stroke' (and, incidentally, this applies whether the stroking is negative or positive). If compliance is stroked, then compliance is what Managers will experience from their subordinates. If they negatively stroke rebellious or passive behaviour then that, too, is what they will get. On the other hand, it is not enough to ignore the behaviour of the other person, as this will most likely be experienced as a negative stroke — the Little Professor in each of us is exceptionally sharp at intuitively understanding ulterior transactions, and very sensitive to the Child feelings in others, however well concealed at a social level.

We are concerned here with an issue of basic attitude and assumptions. It depends absolutely on both persons having trust in themselves and in each other ('I'm OK with me and you are OK with me'). In a situation where the relationship is characterised by symbiosis, the position is one of 'I'm OK with me but you are not OK with me' which is complementary to the position of the other person, 'I am not OK with me but you are OK with me'. In the one case the Parent is active a great deal of the time, controlling and unnecessarily nurturative, and in the other case the Child is unhealthily adapted, seeking continuously to please or defy.

By altering the nature of transactions so that each individual is permitted to use all of himself, and by changing the stroke pattern, we believe much can be done to invite the active co-operation of managers and subordinates with each other, and in addition bring about more effective colleague relationships.

Change seems to be accompanied for most of us by feelings of anxiety. We are invested psychologically in our present way of being and feel reluctant to give up our current assumptions and strategies since they appear to work most of the time. Even when there is evidence to the contrary we may prefer to ignore it or distort it, rather than experiment with new approaches which we are fearful of since we do not know exactly what the consequences will be. This is where the trust issue is critical. Managers, particularly, will need to be willing to take the risk of letting those who work under them function as autonomous beings, and in so doing trust that they will respond from the position 'I'm OK/You're OK'.

They will need, in addition, to be willing to trust themselves, to use their Free Child feelings and their Little Professor intuitions to help them to increase their responsiveness and make decisions, especially in dealing with passivity.

Of course, if alienation, as we have described it here, is to be reduced, it will require an equal amount of effort on the part of subordinates, in the same kind of way. They will need to be willing to risk taking the responsibility of functioning from their own Adult and Parent, and to give up working for strokes for their Adapted Child, trusting that these will be replaced by strokes for being themselves as responsible, autonomous and creative individuals willing to commit themselves freely to co-operate with others for mutual benefit.

Summary

We have suggested that transactional analysis as a descriptive and diagnostic model of organisational behaviour can be used to understand alienation. Many organisational relationships, particularly between levels in the hierarchy, are characterised by a series of Parent to Adapted Child transactions, thereby depriving both the individuals and the organisation of the benefit of, on the one hand, much Child creativity and human warmth, and on the other hand, of much fruitful thinking and responsible problem solving. This we see as due to the functioning of individuals in organisations being less than their full capacity. Not only is there the direct loss of productive collaboration, but, in addition, individuals are likely to feel deprived and thwarted, and are likely then to withdraw energy from work and use it for more or less passive behaviours, thereby increasing the psychological, and sometimes real, gap between management and employees. We are suggesting that if the individual will take responsibility for functioning freely and appropriately with all parts of himself, and, in addition, will be more sensitive to his own and other's stroke needs, much can be done to change the quality of relationships in organisations so that alienation is replaced by committed, caring, co-operation.

References

Argyris, C., *Interpersonal Competence and Organisational Effectiveness* (Irwin-Dorsey, Homewood, 1962).
Blake, R.R. and Mouton, J.S., *The Managerial Grid* (Gulf, Houston, 1964).
Berne, E., *The Structure and Dynamics of Organisations & Groups* (Grove Press,

New York, 1963).
Berne, E., *Games People Play* (Grove Press, New York, 1964).
——, *What do you say after you say hello* (Grove Press, New York, 1972).
Ellis, J., *T.A. Talk* (Child and Family Consultants Inc, Fort Smith, 1974).
Maslow, A.H., *Motivation and Personality* (Harper and Row, New York, 1954).
Mayo, E., *The Human Problems of an Industrial Civilization* (Macmillan, New York, 1933).
McGregor, D., *The Human Side of Enterprise* (McGraw-Hill, New York, 1960).
Mellor, K. and Schiff, E., 'Redefining', *Transactional Analysis Journal*, 1975, 5(3) 303-311.
Piaget, J. *The Lenguage and Thought of the Child*, trans. M. Warden (Harcourt, Brace & World, New York, 1926) (Original French edition 1923).
Schiff, J.G., *Cathexis Reader, Transactional Analysis Treatment of Psychosis* (Harper and Row, New York, 1975).
Steiner, C., *Scripts people live* (Grove Press, New York, 1974).
Wallgren, K.R., 'Managerial Corral', *Transactional Analysis Journal*, 1975, 5(4) 373-375.
Woolams, S., Brown, M. and Huige, K., *Transactional Analysis in Brief* (Huron Valley Institute, Ann Arbor, 1974).

7 MANAGEMENT EDUCATION METHODS FOR HUMANISING THE WORKPLACE

Cary L. Cooper

Preston and Post (1974) described three stages of managerial development, which they refer to as the 'three managerial revolutions'. The first managerial revolution was the appearance of management itself as a specialised function within 'hierarchical organisations'. The second revolution, 'professionalisation', was encouraged by the growth in industrial organisations and the complexity of managerial tasks. The third and contemporary revolution is 'participation'. Participation means, as Preston and Post define it, 'the inclusion of persons and groups involved and concerned with the diverse outcomes of managerial activity as participants in the managerial process'. We see daily examples of the movement toward participation in industrial life, in the form of participative management within organisations, government pressure for greater worker participation in decision-making, worker cooperatives, etc. This third managerial revolution has enormous consequences for the development of management education and training. The questions we would like to focus on in this chapter are: How will the movement toward industrial democracy, participation, and humanisation of the workforce affect the future development of management training? What demands will be placed on management educators to meet the needs of industrial life based on 'participative management'? What resources can management educators draw on to help facilitate the process of humanising worklife?

Before we examine some of the problems associated with *participative management*, it might be useful in the first instance to define the concept. In its broadest possible sense worker participation means wider involvement and participation by a company's employees in the decision-making process of that organisation. There are several important points, however, that must be emphasised about this definition. First, participation in decision-making is meant to include all employees: manual workers, middle management and clerical staff, and not simply the unskilled and skilled worker on the shop floor as is frequently assumed. Second, there is an important distinction between what Strauss and Rosenstein (1970) term *immediate* and *distant* participation. Immediate participation refers to workers' involvement in the day-to-day decision-making process of their work group, be it on the shop floor or among clerical workers in the office. This form of participation, over the last ten years, has manifested itself in the development of autonomous work groups (*à la* Volvo), job enrichment schemes, work restructuring, etc. — in this sense, worker participation in management is seen as a means of improving the quality of the worker's life on the job. Distant participation, on the other hand, refers to the process of including company employees at the top management level of the organisation, so that they may be involved in decision-making on long-term policy issues (e.g. investment, employment, etc.).

From the point of view of management education the problems associated with immediate and distant participation are very similar differing only in degree and orientation. What I would like to do in this chapter is to focus on some of these problems and issues and attempt to speculate on what we might do in the way of training and education to begin to deal with them.

Educating managers

One of the very first problems that we will have to overcome if we are truly to develop more humanising work environments is to educate not only the existing first line and middle managers but also the senior managers to accept this changing role of management. As Hebden and Shaw (1976) suggest 'the fact is that the participation issue is a challenge to many deep-rooted ideas about the nature of authority and the way leadership should be exercised in organisations'. Participation in the decision-making process of enterprises, at all levels, cannot be legislated or imposed, it will require a process of education and attitude change unparalleled in recent industrial history. Existing managers will have to acquire two different sets of skills. First, the social or human relations skills required of a participative managerial style: facilitating uninhibited information sharing, encouraging shared decision-making and responsibility, understanding one's own needs and behaviour in an effort to avoid creating dependency relationships with subordinates, etc. This will necessitate learning opportunities not only in understanding managerial needs and motivations but also in acquiring the skills associated with facilitating mutual decision-making. Social skill acquisition will be particularly relevant during the interim period of participative management, since this changing managerial approach is likely to develop in the context of the current hierarchical organisational structure. In the longer term this form of training may be less necessary as a new generation of trained managers emerge with different expectations of the work environment which should be consistent with the tenets of the 'third managerial revolution'. The transition period is likely to be long and tortuous and will require all the facilities, skills, and resources we can muster. There are, however, a wide variety of management training methods (Cooper, 1973) currently available that could be adapted to meet the problems arising during this transition period. Many of the group dynamics, interpersonal and interactive skills programmes could be used to lay the groundwork for the acquisition of these sorts of skills and indeed could provide the platform for the exploration and change of formerly held attitudes and the acceptance of new attitudes based on this ideology (Cooper, 1976).

Second, as more decision-making power devolves to the working unit, the manager, together with his work group colleagues, will have to develop the skills that will keep them working effectively as a team — skills at being able to resolve task and interpersonal differences, being able to negotiate work roles within the group, etc. In the short term this might be best done by a group specialist or consultant brought in from outside, who would help the work group to explore and utlise more fully the available human resources and build self-maintaining systems.

As we move increasingly toward 'group cell technology' and as we try and encourage communal or work-group decision-making, the problems associated with interpersonal relations and dynamics must inevitably grow and become magnified. This will require the skills that group training specialists have been cultivating for the last two decades; skills in identifying and resolving interpersonal blockages, in helping to build 'trusting/caring' work groups, and in encouraging inter-dependency — which involves encouraging mutual cooperation, effective decision-making, and the creation of a group structure that is adapted to the individual's needs. These are skills which may be best learned by the work group as a whole in the first instance, in consultation with team development specialists (e.g. management consultants, government-based change agents, etc.). Later the group should be able to develop its own mechanisms for dealing with these sorts of conflicts and inevitable consequences of 'sharing' decision-making and other responsibilities. In some groups they may decide that this task will be the function of the manager, in others somebody else may take this role on (somebody the group feels has greater skills in that area). This raises an even more fundamental problem about participative management in general, that is, if we are going to rely increasingly on blue and white collar workers at all levels to decide on matters concerning their work, who should appoint the manager or 'work group facilitator' (as it may be called in the future) in the first place? On one extreme you could allow the work unit to decide the roles of all its members, on the other, management could decide unilaterally that a particular individual will have overall coordinating responsibility, leaving it up to this individual in conjunction with his work group to clarify roles and functions together. This is a problem that permeates the whole area of participative management, the *degree* of involvement of the workers in the decision-making function. In the figure below Kenneth Walker highlights the differing degrees to which workers can influence managerial functions.

Management decides unilaterally without prior information to workers	Management decides unilaterally but workers are informed before decision is put into effect	Management decides after hearing workers' views	Negotiations take place but management goes ahead if no agreement is reached	Negotiations take place and no action is taken without agreement	Workers decide unilaterally

Source: Walker, K., 'Workers' Participation in Management — Problems, Practice and Prospects', IILS Bulletin, 1973.

It seems to me that management will be forced more and more to accept the position that some of their former prerogatives will have to be forfeited and they will have to move increasingly from the centre of the above figure to the right. Where a particular organisation will be along this continuum, will depend on the individual workers and managers involved. It would be unwise and even foolish to attempt to suggest that all companies should let the workers decide unilaterally all decisions, when we all know that each organisation is unique, located in a specific industry with specific problems, composed of workers whose needs may be different from other workers, etc. Some workers and indeed managers may require more or less structure than others, may desire more or less decision-making power, may prefer more or less varied job, etc. A flexible approach to a managerial style consistent with the organisation culture will be required for effective utilisation of participative management.

Educating workers

The skills necessary to be able to do this leads us to a third area of 'educational need' which is the training and development of the workers' managerial skills. Any movement along the above continuum from roughly the centre to the right will necessitate the acquisition of technical, social and power skills for the worker as well as the existing managers. First, if workers are to be or to possess the capability of being in more and more activities of the enterprise they will need to increase their knowledge of what Walker (1973) describes as the 'productive tasks' of the organisation, 'the task dimension is concerned with their activities as agents in the production process, meeting certain task-requirements arising from the function performed by the enterprise'. If workers are to form part of an effective decision-making team at any level in the organisation (e.g. from the shop floor to the Board) they will need to know something about basic economics, the economics of their particular industry, the psychology of group behaviour and decision-making, work design, organisation theory and structure, wage determination, fiscal and pricing policy and a host of other traditional management science subjects. The ILO held a symposium on economic education for trade unionists (ILO, 1974) in which they emphasised that it was essential for greater industrial democracy and participation that education 'provide a critical knowledge of economic facts that will help all workers to actively achieve understanding of the problems they are facing and to participate in decisions and action aimed at their solution'. They outlined a number of basic questions regarding education one might consider both in terms of various levels of needs and in determining 'possible educational methods suitable for study, training and research'. Although they were orientated toward economic education primarily, many of these questions generically phrased would apply equally to worker education for participative management generally: *general questions* — should management education be selective and designed to serve the functional needs of particular workers or their representatives, what types of training could be envisaged in respect of various levels of needs, how do we determine which are the most important and effective training programmes, etc.; *responsibility for the education process* — should the trade unions or other public authorities mobilise the educational resources for this educational process and, if the latter, through what institutions, who should influence the choice of course content; *course organisation and methods* — what is a suitable length for a training programme, should it be on-the-job training or in an academic institutional context, what criteria should be used to select themes for study, how can the content best be related to the experiences of the learner, should any particular methods be especially recommended or avoided (e.g. lectures, group work, case studies, etc.), should any special training for teachers involved in these programmes be offered, etc. These and many other questions will have to be asked and satisfactorily answered in developing effective technical education for rank-and-file workers.

In terms of developing the social skills of shop floor workers, shop stewards, etc. there are a number of different types of skills of working with people which may be useful. Berger and Harrison (1976) outline the types of interpersonal skills that are needed in work groups:

(i) Communication: Competence in the ability to listen, draw others out, develop *rapport*, and to be brief and concise.

(ii) Leadership and Influence: Competence in identifying different approaches to leadership and in choosing an appropriate style for managing in a given situation. Competence to organise and influence others in order to achieve objectives. Ability to understand how people become motivated to work effectively.

(iii) Decision-making and Problem-solving: Competence in working toward quality decisions and commitment to their implementations.

A wide variety of social skill training activities are readily available to do this sort of education job, they have been used successfully with managers for well over a decade (Smith, 1976) and, indeed, they have also been used on a more limited basis with shop-floor workers as well (Cooper and Oddie, 1972). The educational methods in this area of skill development are available, the important task here is to identify for each different group of worker which of the interpersonal/interactive skills outlined above are more appropriate for the functions they will be performing. The point here is that the social skills required of worker directors on the Board of a company may be different in emphasis and scope than those required by members of an autonomous work group or those participating in a job enrichment scheme.

It may also be important for workers to learn about the nature of power and develop skills in the use of power. Power has negative connotations because it is usually associated with negative behaviour but as King and Glidewell (1976) suggest it is an essential ingredient of almost all human relationships, particularly for work group relationships. Walker (1972) suggests that 'the power dimension is concerned with their activities as individuals and groups possessing certain interest, which they seek to advance and protect in a manner that provides them with a satisfactory net gain? The acquisition of information and skill in this area would require an understanding of the various sources of power; knowledge, resources (money, manpower, etc.), social pressure, authority, law, norms and values, personal style (e.g. charisma, strong dependence), and coercion (King and Glidewell, 1976). There are both didactive (Schelling, 1970) and experiential (Oshry, 1972) techniques currently available which could be used to work on the issues and skills inherent in understanding the nature of power — they may have to be adapted to focus on participative management but the educational foundations are there and the potential unlimited.

Training the humanisers

In addition to meeting the requisite educational needs of the managers and workers in organisations who will be on the front line of increasing efforts at participative management, we will need to prepare those who will be designing and aiding these future developments; the personnel and industrial relations specialists, internal change agents within the organisation (e.g. OD consultants), engineers and planners, accountants, etc. As Davis and Cherns (1976) suggest, 'these persons will require training tailored to their roles as planners, evaluators, and developers of criteria of organisational and individual effectiveness, whose decisions will determine day-to-day life in the workplace'. It is particularly important that adequate training is provided for these service functions, since they will be so central to any change programme in this area. After all, it can be argued (Davis and Cherns, 1976), these people will 'influence policy through the methods they use, the effects they choose to measure or ignore, and the advice they give'. The training of engineers in understanding the implications of shopfloor technology design, for example, is a particularly important development if we are to build workplace environments of the future which will minimise the stresses of our current technology, enable greater effective man-machine interface, and provide the socio-technical climate for greater participative management. On the education of these functions within organisations will depend the future of any efforts to 'reconceptualise man's relationship to work and organisational life' and to enhance the quality of working life. It is hoped that universities, other institutions of higher education, and the relevant professional associations will take it on themselves to provide this educational service to these specialists. The stakes are too high for them to back out of this challenge.

Organisational change

Management education should not only devote its time and effort to preparing (through changing attitudes and increasing relevant information and knowledge) the existing manager (first line to senior) and rank-and-file worker for participative management but also begin to develop the organisation culture and structure as well. Lippitt (1969) sees the successful organisational unit or work team as having the following characteristics:

> An understanding of a commitment to common goals.
>
> The integration of resources of as wide as possible a range of team members, so as to use their contributions and increase their sense of ownership and commitment.
>
> The ability and willingness to analyse and review team processes.
>
> Trust and openness in communications and relationships.
>
> A strong sense of belonging by its members.

Beckhard (1969) has a similar set of foci and objectives to organisational development; establishing goals or priorities, analysing and distributing the work, examining how the group works (procedures, processes, norms), and examining the relationships among the group members as they work. Mangham (1976) has suggested that there are three fundamentally different approaches in preparing organisational units, be they work groups or larger units such as divisions, to begin to work more participatively. The first approach is through low structure learning events. 'This model more clearly approaches the T-group proper in that it requires people to attend off-site for several days and in that it focuses upon here-and-now behaviour within the group as its prime source of data. As the event develops, the learning is increasingly related to the work situation and the nature of the everyday problems faced by them in that setting.' This approach is primarily focussed on interpersonal relations within the work group or organisational unit (frequently between the boss and subordinates) and is limited in that it is not task- or action-orientated. The second approach is through semi-structured organisational development programmes. Here a consultant works with the organisational unit before, during and after the learning process. This process involves seven stages: entry, data collection, sensitisation, feedback, priority-setting, action, and follow-up. In this approach an internal or external consultant is working with the organisational unit or work group to lay the foundations of the learning or educational experience to achieve greater participation and involvement in the decision-making process. This requires mutually setting of goals, collecting and sharing information about the functioning of the work group, setting priorities for discussion, problem-solving and planning of action strategies based on the shared data and agreed priorities, and following up the consequences of the changes to ensure that the needs of the group are being met, that participation and involvement in work is taking place.

And finally, a third approach could be through the more structured team building and organisational change programme, such as Blake and Mouton's (1969) Grid, Coverdale training, Redden's matrix, etc. These are well-planned, structured learning experiences that build sequentially through a series of phases. For example, the Grid approach to organisational development begins with one week stranger groups working together on issues such as team organisation, communication, commitment, planning, decision-making, etc., where the focus is on building on strengths and overcoming barriers to effective participation and involvement. The second phase of the Grid begins to focus on *actual* work groups, frequently starting from the top and working its way down the organisation. The purpose of this phase is to encourage a work group to examine its processes, the way it works together, its style and approach to management, etc. With slight modification and differences in emphasis this approach to organisational development could be used successfully in encouraging greater participative management at all levels. In the past it has concentrated, in the main, on management development but it has the capability to go beyond that.

The educational system

The educational processes associated with developing participative management will have to extend beyond the work involvement in the longer term, if it is to inculcate in the young the attitudes and values associated with humanising the workplace. In Western society there is a very strong bias in the formal education system to internalise in school age children the values of competition, individualism, greater mobility and increased individual status. If we would like to move toward more humanising work environments, ones based on collective decision-making and responsibility, open communications, mutual support, etc., then we will have to start the educational process very early indeed, in the schools. As Hoyt (1972) suggested, 'society has charged education to teach youngsters to work, (and) about work and the working world'. Reubens (1974) has offered some of the following recommendations about changes needed in American schools to improve the subsequent quality of working life for today's students, particularly as regards vocational education: (a) highest priorities in high school education should be the improvement of basic communications, inculcation of good work attitudes, and orientation to the work world (b) work-study and cooperative education programmes should be greatly expanded, as a means both of easing the move from school to full-time job and of the final years of school more bearable for non-academic youth and more relevant for the others. Implicit in Reubens' suggestions is that school age children will be able to formulate more realistic attitudes and values about work from direct experience, attitudes which may be dissonant with those currently being conveyed in the formal educational system. MacMichael (1974) summarises the occupational bias in formal education '... the old middle class ethic and the associated value system may no longer be appropriate to the emerging economy. There is evidence that a new value system is developing especially among the youth of the American middle class, that is more appropriate, particularly with regards to occupational status. It is questionable whether the school system, which as presently constituted is the institutional embodiment of the traditional middle class value system, can do other than it has done, that is, encourage 'upward' mobility toward 'higher status' jobs ...'

Conclusion

In summary, anyone working in industry in the UK can't help but be concerned about the deterioration in industrial relations, the growing rigidity in management/worker roles, the lack of mutual understanding and communication, the concern with winning battles, the absence of genuine efforts at the long-term resolution of problems. Often we hear of stoppages or strikes starting from what the public would regard as trivial issues unrelated to the simple demand for a higher wage — such issues as demarcation disputes, or even the rearranging of holiday schedules. These catalytic incidents are not the central foundations of grievances, but frequently rather the symptoms of difficulties between people at work, difficulties in the style and approach to the management of worklife. It is essential for our own 'survival' and 'satisfaction at work' that we do something about the way we manage the workplace; that we change attitudes, that we encourage participation and involvement, that we reduce worker alienation. One of the main conclusions by Davis and Trist (1974) about improving the quality of working life sums this up succinctly:

> self regulation and control at the workplace through autonomous or semi-autonomous jobs and groups yield high levels of satisfaction, self-development, and learning and high performance in output and quality. They form the basis for further organizational design to reduce the repressive and coercive character of organizations and resulting worker alienation.

References

Beckhard, R., *Organizational Development* (Addison-Wesley, New York, 1969).
Berger, M. and Harrison, K., 'A New Approach to Interpersonal Skills Development' in C.L. Cooper, *Developing Social Skills in Managers* (Macmillan, London, 1976).
Blake, R. and Mouton, J., *Building a Dynamic Corporation through Grid Organizational Development* (Addison-Wesley, New York, 1969).
Cooper, C.L. and Oddie, H., *An Evaluation of Two Approaches to Social Skill Training in the Catering Industry* (Hotel and Catering Industry Training Board, London, 1972).
Cooper, C.L., *Group Training for Individual and Organizational Development* (S. Karger, Basle, Switzerland, 1973).
———, *Developing Social Skills in Managers* (Macmillan, London, 1976).
Davis, L.E. and Trist, E., 'Improving the Quality of Work Life' in J. O'Toole, *Work and the Quality of Life* (MIT Press, Mass., 1974).
Hebden, J. and Shaw, G., 'Pitfalls in Participation', *Management Today*, (January 1976), 68-88.
Hoyt, K.B., 'Education as Preparation for Employment' in *Technology and the American Economy* (US Government Printing Office, Washington, 1972).
International Labour Office, 'Symposium on Economic Education for Trade Unionists' (Geneva, 1974).
King, D.C. and Glidewell, J.C., 'Power' in Pfeiffer and Jones *1976 Annual Handbook for Group Facilitators*, 139-142.
Lippitt, G., *Optimizing Human Resources* (Addison-Wesley, New York, 1971).
MacMichael, D.C., 'Occupational Bias in Formal Education and Its Effect on Preparing Children for Work' in J. O'Toole, *Work and the Quality of Work* (MIT Press, Mass., 1974).
Mangham, I.L., 'Team Development in Industry' in C.L. Cooper, *Developing Social Skills in Managers*, (Macmillan, London, 1976).
Oshry, B., 'Power and the Power Lab' in W. Warner Burke, *Contemporary Organization Development* (NTL Institute, Washington, 1972).
Preston, L.E. and Post, J.E., 'The Third Managerial Revoltuion', *Academy of Management Journal*, 1974 17 (3), 476-486.
Reubens, B.G., 'Vocational Education for *All* in High School' in J. O'Toole, *Work and Quality of Life* (MIT Press, Mass., 1974).
Schelling, T.C., *The Strategy of Conflict* (Harvard University Press, Boston, 1970).
Smith, P.B., 'Why Successful Groups Succeed' in C.L. Cooper, *Developing Social Skills in Managers* (Macmillan, London, 1976).

Strauss, G. and Rosenstein, E., 'Worker participation: a critical view', *Industrial Relations* (1970) 9, 197-214.
Walker, K.F., 'Workers' Participation in Management — Problems, Practice, and Prospects', *International Institute for Labour Studies Bulletin* (1973) Number 12, 3-35.

8 NEW MANAGEMENT ATTITUDES TO THE HUMANISATION OF WORK

J.N. Watson

It is no part of the writer's intention in this chapter to describe in detail the variety of ways in which companies of the Royal Dutch/ Shell Group are trying to humanise the workplace. For one thing, to do so would be to produce a catalogue of activities in the fields of organisation development, training, employee relations, remuneration, health, safety and so on which would fail to address the deeper issues with which this book is concerned. For another, the task would be impossibly complex: there are over a thousand companies in the Group, differing greatly in size, complexity and environmental circumstances, and their organisational cultures, of course, exhibit a similar degree of diversity.

It is not difficult to understand, therefore, that in spite of the fact that all these companies draw freely upon the specialist resources of the Group Service Companies in London and The Hague, there are substantial differences in the attitudes of their managements to matters such as the humanisation of work, and there is no clear-cut Group policy on the subject. Shell companies, however, have been working in various aspects of this field for a number of years, and the rest of this chapter, after a passing glance at the origins of our interest in these matters, will develop the somewhat controversial theme that the organisation in which people feel fulfilled by their work may also be highly effective in the performance of its chosen tasks. We shall then look at some of the characteristics of such organisations, and at some of the obstacles to their development.

The writer is responsible for the co-ordination of organisation development work in Shell, but the opinions and attitudes he expresses in this chapter are not necessarily shared by the managers with whom he works.

The collapse of authority

A distinguished American OD consultant, Professor Charles K. Ferguson of UCLA, tells the story of a senior manager who is alleged to have said: 'I wouldn't have any difficulty with all this ambiguity —

if only someone would explain it to me!' One cannot help sympathising with the chap. He was merely putting into words the uneasiness that is widely felt today by many people in authority — an ill-defined suspicion that they are no longer wholly able to discharge their managerial tasks to their own satisfaction, let alone to that of others.

The trouble seems to have started about twenty years ago. Joe Kelly, of the Department of Management at Concordia University, Montreal, has said:

> Probably in the mid-Fifties . . . Things started to go awry. The roles were still there but the relations began to change. Children started cheeking parents, patients suing their doctors, students chasing presidents out of their offices and smoking their cigars . . . Suddenly the rule of law and order began to crumble and with it, credibility.[1]

This questioning of authority began to make itself evident about the same time in industry, and classical symptoms of poor organisational health like growing absenteeism and increased labour turnover began to alarm industrial managements in many countries. The companies of the Royal Dutch/Shell Group were no exception, and it rapidly became evident to many Shell managers that the values, attitudes and management styles that had served them well in the past were being called increasingly into question by their employees and by society at large. Some of these managers enlisted the help of psychologists and social scientists in connection with their problems, and the hunt was on for answers to a variety of questions that are now, two decades or so later, grouped under the interrelated headings of quality of working life (QWL), social responsibility and organisation development (OD).

It is this interrelationship that makes it difficult to discuss the humanisation of the workplace as a single subject. The quality of working life cannot be measured solely in terms of financial reward, working conditions and the like — though these are obviously very important. There is something in the nature of man that transcends such things, and for many people makes it imperative that the work they do and the quality of their contribution commands the approval of the society of which they feel themselves to be a part. The trends of recent years, in fact, suggest that unless our human institutions offer those who work in them the opportunity to satisfy these basic needs they may find it difficult to survive in the longer term.

On the question of changing values Carl Rogers, of the Center for Studies of the Person in La Jolla, California, talking about the New Man he sees emerging in the United States, says:

> It seems ... that this person of tomorrow is deeply concerned with living in a moral and ethical way, but the morals are new and shifting, the ethics are relative to the situation, and the one thing that is not tolerated is a discrepancy between verbal standards and the actual living of values.[2]

If Rogers is right it follows that the standards expected of our employees in their working lives should be consistent with those they maintain as private citizens: if the nature of the work of an organisation and the ways in which it seeks to do it conflict with these values the enterprise may be heading for trouble. Not every employee, of course, is so punctilious, or wants greater responsibility and challenge in his job, but there appear to be millions who do. We believe that if we can develop our human institutions in such a way that the people in them share in the decision-making to a degree that accords fairly well with their competence and aspirations we shall have overcome the biggest barrier to the humanisation of work. It should be borne in mind, too, that the workplace to be humanised is not only that of the worker on the shop floor: managers are human, too, and alienation and frustration can occur at any level.

Whether or not organisations that exhibit this degree of participative decision-making are likely to be more effective is still open to debate. One of the central problems is that traditional criteria or organisational efficiency are based on a very different set of values, in which return on investment is paramount. There exists today a wide spectrum of attitudes to monetary profit. At one end it is seen as the only objective and at the other as an operating constraint.

The whole question of performance criteria is in the melting pot. Many organisations are experimenting with human asset accounting, total asset accounting, social balance sheets and the like. These are all attempts, however, to describe the functioning of the organisation in short term financial statistics, and it seems to the writer that they may be little more than interim steps towards the eventual establishment of more radical criteria. However this may be, it seems clear that for some time to come many of our efforts to humanise the workplace will depend to some extent on acts of faith on the part of those who have the power to make the relevant decisions.

The question of power in this sense is critical. The symptoms of alienation are apparent to a greater or lesser degree in most of our large institutions. The dilemma of the industrial manager is paralleled in government, in the trades unions, in the church, and in hospitals, prisons, universities and schools. The use and misuse of power is the central issue in our current preoccupations with the rights of minorities, women and even children. The clamour for a share in the decision-making process is deafening on every hand.

Here our pursuit of the keys to the humanisation of work lands us squarely in the territory of organisation development. It is clear that our institutions are not working to the satisfaction of the majority, and the majority is now considerably more powerful (as well as vociferous) than it used to be. It is also clear that we are not dealing with a party political issue because the problems we are addressing arise both in the public and private enterprise sectors of the economies of many countries. We are driven accordingly to look for ways of improving the functioning of the organisations we have built to enable us to run our affairs.

J.W.L. Adams, of the Administrative Staff College, Henley, has given a simple but attractive definition of organisation: 'The task of organisation is to create the conditions in which people can behave effectively.'[3] If this is a good definition, we have to ask ourselves a number of fundamental questions — What is our central purpose? Who are our people and what are their values, skills and aspirations? How can we employ their unused capacities? Should we modify our technology? Does society want us to do what we are doing?

The rigorous examination of questions such as these is a big job. The answers lie partly with the people in the enterprise itself, and partly in the world outside it, and we may find that we need expert assistance to help us to clarify them, because they are partly dependent on subjective judgements, and differ from one organisation to the next.

Organisations cannot be represented satisfactorily in two dimensions. The classical organisation chart, with its associated mandates and job descriptions, is little more than a skeleton of the real thing. Two organisations that look similar on paper may be no more alike than two families.

It is this uniqueness about any given organisation that militates against global solutions in the field of OD and in efforts to humanise the work of our employees. What appears to be a considerable improvement in one organisational unit is frequently a failure in another that appears to be similar. There may be gains, especially in terms of overall learning, but transplants of this sort are usually disappointing.

There are probably three main reasons for this. First, the people in the two organisations are different, and there will inevitably be perceptible differences in their attitudes, aspirations, and so on. Second, their environments and their communications with them are unlikely to be identical. Third, there is the matter of psychological commitment to change. It has been shown again and again that unless sufficient time and effort are devoted to enabling the people in each new organisation to work their own way through their perceptions of the issues, their commitment to change — or even to the need for change — will not develop to the level which is necessary for a reasonable measure of success.

Considerations of this kind, amongst others, have led to the demise of the old style organisation consultant, whose stock-in-trade was a variety of 'scientific' prescriptions based largely on his previous experience in other organisations, and who has a lot to answer for in many cases in terms of helping to dehumanise our workplaces. Such prescriptions are often unacceptable to those for whom they are written. The main thrust of most of the OD efforts in Shell companies, including what is being done where less challenging jobs are concerned, is towards helping managers and their employees to examine their work and its relation to a variety of external factors so that they themselves can suggest better ways of doing things.

Organising for tomorrow

The kind of organisational cultures that we are seeking to establish in our confusing new world are amongst other things adventurous, flexible, heuristic, and socially responsible. In general we need organisational climates in which people will be able to play their individual parts in grasping new opportunities, combating threats, and above all experiencing their work as useful, challenging and enjoyable.

By an adventurous culture we mean one in which it is no longer acceptable to go on replicating the past. It is a cliché today to say that the world is changing with ever-increasing speed, especially in terms of social expectations. In large institutions, with their multiplicity of specialised functions and co-ordinating mechanisms, it is necessary to be constantly on the alert to avoid excessive compartmentalisation and the encapsulation of ideas and procedures, and to ensure that the formal and informal systems of reward and punishment that exist in all organisations allow a reasonable degree of risk-taking by people at every level.

The writer believes that there is a good deal of scope for management education and research in the matter of the nature of change in human institutions. Many managers declare their willingness to accept change 'provided we know where it is going to lead', but there is surely something tautological about the notion of a change that has wholly predictable results. Real change, of the kind going on in society today, seems to call for a response that is something more than just another programme from the old repertoire, and for a readiness to make decisions while a fair measure of uncertainty still exists.

This brings us to the topic of creativity in organisations. A number of creative techniques, mostly of the brainstorming type, have been fairly widely used for a good number of years. One of the essentials for success with such methods is that the temptations to analyse and evaluate during the creative phase must be rigorously suppressed. Evaluation comes later, when the inspiration has dried up.

The writer believes that this is appropriate behaviour not only in the rarified atmosphere of the creative laboratory but also in day-to-day business at all levels of management. There are obvious limits to the chances a responsible manager can take, but the adventurous organisations we need today call for a greater readiness to make managerial acts of faith than has usually been considered desirable in the past. We believe that in such a culture it is possible for the worker to develop greater pride in his work, and for the manager to display humility in his, to the ultimate benefit of everyone concerned.

To be adventurous, in organisational terms, is not the same thing as to be flexible. Flexibility implies the capacity to respond according to the needs of the moment, and includes the possibilities of being cautious as well as adventurous, bureaucratic as well as organic, authoritarian as well as participative, and so on. For organisations to develop and retain the ability to move effortlessly back and forth along such continua is not easy, but it can be helpful in this respect to focus on the performance of specific activities, rather than on jobs or roles. This is not the same thing as matrix working, being much more loosely structured, and it differs from the use of project groups or task forces because it is usually concerned with the activity in question over a comparatively long period of time, and because people can move into and out of the group as required (and often at their own initiative).

Norske Shell, in Norway, is a good example of an organisation in which activity working has been developed, a man being able to act as an expert resource to one of his colleagues in a given area of the latter's responsibility while in another activity their roles are reversed. This sort of working has several obvious advantages, notably that it tends to increase understanding across functional barriers, usually enriches decision-making, and makes on the whole for more challenging jobs and better possibilities for self-development. It appears, moreover, to be as effective at lower levels as at higher ones.

As in project working, it is left to the person with the prime responsibility for the activity in question to negotiate for the assistance he requires from others, but it is not uncommon for someone to ask to be included in the group when he feels he has a contribution to make. It has also been our experience, on the whole, that the obvious danger of creating a culture in which everyone is dabbling in everyone else's business does not materialise, probably because the dynamics of the groups themselves tend to 'freeze out' the ineffectual contributor.

The healthy organisation, like the healthy animal, is constantly adapting itself to its environment. This adaptation requires awareness and some ability to learn. We want to increase the capacity of our organisations to learn how to learn from our own experiences and from those of others. Our starting points, of course, are our people — warts and all — and their existing tasks. By helping our employees to develop the habit of reconsidering what they are doing in terms of the feedback they receive about their work from various sources we are building cybernetic and heuristic elements into our organisational way of life, and trying to perpetuate and develop those we already have.

The relevance of this to QWL lies in carrying this process as near to the operational level as possible. Classical organisations had their cybernetic qualities too, but the feedback loops were very long and the responses often slow. In the modern world every employee is a potential receiver of feedback from many points in his complex environment, and we want this feedback to be examined and acted upon when necessary by the shortest reasonable route. This does not mean that we want every worker to make all the decisions that affect his work without consulting anyone else. What it does mean is that we want him to assume as much responsibility as he feels able to, and to consult others as required. We find that behavioural pressures from peers and adjacent levels of supervision can for the most part be relied upon to exert the necessary restraining influences, and we feel that the possibilities of increased overall effectiveness and of QWL gains for our employees usually justify the risks.

The social responsibility of business, and especially of multinational business, has become the focus of one of the great debates of our time. The subject has many aspects, and is approached in a variety of ways by different institutions, but we see in QWL work a new dimension, and a key one at that, in our efforts to help companies all over the world to behave like useful and responsible members of the societies in which they conduct their business. Shell managers in general are expected to balance the interests of the consumer, the employee, the investor and the rest of the community in their decision-making, and to the extent that they are able to improve their organisations to make better use of the capacities of the employees we believe that the other sectors of society will also benefit in the long run.

The socially responsible company, of course, must turn its face outwards to society, and OD work is very helpful in this respect because employees are also citizens. By involving them increasingly in decisions about their work we are effectively increasing the attention we pay to the attitudes, requirements and sanctions of the societies around us.

Some mythological obstacles

We have considered in the foregoing some of the organisational characteristics that the writer regards as having an important bearing in today's conditions on increasing the effectiveness and enjoyment of work. These characteristics represent, however, a substantial shift in business values over a comparatively short time, and there are a number of myths more or less deeply embedded in Western business culture that tend to militate against their development. The reader may have come across some or all of them in his own working environment.

By far the most powerful of these implants is the myth of scientific management, which, as we have already noted, has recently gone into a rapid decline along with scientific consulting. The trouble with this sort of management is not that it is scientific — indeed, we sorely need managers who respect the rigorous fact-finding, analysis, hypothesising and testing against reality that characterises the classical scientific method — but that it is esoteric and over-prescriptive. It presupposes that the behaviour of those managed can generally be predicted, and that the decision-makers have sufficient information, wisdom and skills at their disposal to make further consultation unnecessary. Both premises, in our challenging world, are being called increasingly into question, and in addition, as we have said earlier, it is becoming apparent that the psychological commitment engendered in the employee by involving him in making a decision is often at least as important as the quality of the decision itself. In fact, as those with experience of this kind of employee participation will probably testify: the decision is qualitatively enriched by the employee's up-to-date and detailed knowledge and experience, and his emotional and intellectual support are forthcoming because of his involvement.

It is not an easy thing for managers trained in the business world of twenty years ago to relinquish the prescriptive style. Most European managers, at least, have modelled their behaviour on the decision-making norms of the colonial services, the landowning classes, the armed forces, the Church and the other professions. The entrepreneurial nature of business, however, made it different and slightly disreputable. 'No gentleman enters commerce!', thundered the European aristocrats a hundreds years ago.

The interaction of these powerful traditions produced in the first half of the present century a management paradigm that was highly professional and paternalistic. The role of the manager was clear. He must know more about the business than his employees, and he must treat them well. In return they must work hard at their allotted tasks and be loyal to the undertaking. The authority of the manager, and the employees' lack of it, were accepted almost without question.

For a time the system worked well, in many cases generating great wealth and prestige for the enterprises and nations in which it could develop. But when the values on which it was based began to be eroded by the gradual redistribution of wealth, education and opportunity neither the power nor the omniscience of the manager, however benevolent, could remain unchallenged for long.

Today's managers are squarely in the middle of the ensuing dilemma. What is the real function of management in the last quarter of the 20th century? To whom is the manager responsible? How much participation can an organisation stand before it collapses? How long, on the other hand, can it survive without such a culture?

The writer believes that managers themselves can find answers to these difficult questions, but it will require hard work, optimism, humility and some sort of vision of justice. The answers may differ from culture to culture and change over time, but they are implicit in the basic objectives of our human institutions, and in some cases they are slowly and painfully beginning to emerge. It is becoming clear, for example, that there is a sense in which managers, without abdicating their essential strategic planning and co-ordinating roles, are also serving their workers, managing the boundaries of the organisational systems for which they are responsible and ensuring that these boundaries remain permeable with respect to other related systems within the enterprise and outside it.

In simple terms this means that the manager must not only try to ensure that his organisation has clear objectives, suitable people, an open culture, excellent equipment and the like, but that he must also see that the systems with which it is interdependent are supplying satisfactory data and materials to his operations, and that they are receiving in return the output they require at the lowest cost consistent with the interests of employees, investors (if any) and society at large. This in turn implies that management information systems and other communications must also be excellent.

The foregoing does not seem to us to diminish the importance of the management task today, but it does reinforce the idea that it has to be shared amongst more people. We are seeing in effect the development of a new concept of management — as a function rather than as a cadre — in which the decision-making power is diffused much more widely throughout the organisation than before, with a consequent increase in the day-to-day challenges for the people at lower levels and the possibility (if they care to grasp it) for those at the top to devote more time to the strategic issues that they alone can handle.

The implications for institutionalised work are exciting. The abolition of the power distance between manager and managed could remove an unnecessary strain on both, and could thereby liberate energy and creativity that has been bottled up for too long.

We are talking here, of course, about a general pattern of management over time, and not about emergency situations. No-one in his right mind advocates exhaustive consultation when the building is on fire, but authoritarian management is less likely to be regarded as acceptable after the emergency has passed.

Another well established myth in Western business culture has been that of the economies of scale. Does every department in the organisation use rubber bands? Then we must set up a central rubber band control unit. For a long time it seemed to make sense: one expert, one set of supply contacts, centralised stock records, bulk purchase discounts and the rest. It is probably only in the last fifteen years or so that we have begun to see that the pursuit of such economics, so attractive in terms of the savings in direct costs, may in many cases be involving us in indirect costs of disturbing magnitude.

Why can't we get rubber bands quickly any more? Why does no-one want the rubber band job? Why does no-one understand how important the management of rubber bands has become in this day and age? The wails of despair can be heard loudly and clearly at most of the interfaces where the relentless pursuit of the economies of scale have led us to an excessive degree of specialisation, compartmentalisation and the alienation of one organisational unit from another. Salesmen are regarded by finance control staff as irresponsible opportunists; finance clerks are seen by sales staff as faceless bureaucrats. Personnel specialists think of busy operational managers as robber barons, and are considered to be irrelevant for their pains. Production men hate maintenance engineers, and vice versa. Consultants who specialise in the resolution of conflict are observed to be prospering on all sides.

In some Shell companies OD work has begun to reverse these trends towards excessive specialisation. Financial control units have been reintegrated within sales organisations, and chemical plants have been reorganised so that technological departments now service operational departments instead of conducting technological operations in their own right. Personnel specialists have been moved into management teams of the functions they serve while retaining a species of matrix relationship with the central personnel organisation. To those who suspect that this may be only the swing of the pendulum, it can only be said that at present these arrangements seemed to be desirable, that they appear to be an improvement, and that if at a later date there are indications that they should be changed again our managements will presumably change them. We still seek, of course, to retain the economies of scale where they produce greater effectiveness, but we want to make sure that they are genuine economies, as seen by the people who experience the effects of them in their daily work. We do not abhor bureaucracy — the world needs large administrative organisations — but we aim to ensure that there is a continuing dialogue of high quality between the bureaucratic elements in our organisations and the operational units with which they are interdependent, and we look to that dialogue to minimise the inter-departmental alienation that has grown in recent years to be such a disturbing feature of institutional life.

It is also comparatively recently that we have begun to be aware of the myth of technological determinism, to realise the extent to which the tasks of our employees in their various workplaces have been conditioned by the implications of the technologies we choose. The oil industry, of course, has a number of sophisticated technologies of its own, and in many of its aspects is highly capital intensive. Modern oil refineries and chemical plants, for example, are run by staffs that seem to the outsider to be very small. With ever-growing automation, however, and higher standards of education in the world's work forces, it becomes increasingly important for social reasons as well as considerations of efficiency to re-examine our assumptions about technology. It has been convincingly demonstrated in a number of countries, including the United Kingdom, Norway, Sweden and the United States, that once the so-called 'requirements' of technology cease to be regarded as unquestionable a variety of new and interesting possibilities for working begin to emerge.

The basis of what is now called socio-technical work structuring is that rigorous analysis of the technical as well as the social systems in an organisation often presents opportunities for changing either or both so that the product of their interaction becomes more effective. In some cases, of course, the costs of modifying the technical systems are prohibitive, but in others these costs are likely to be more than counterbalanced by savings elsewhere — typically in reduced turn-over, scrap rates and supervision. This kind of work is usually done, against organsational objectives, by teams of managers supported by experienced OD consultants, but workers at lower levels have also been involved quite successfully, especially in Scandinavia.

It is extremely important in socio-technical redesign to make sure that the possible effects on other organisations are taken fully into account. Many socio-technical developments have failed to fulfil their promise because the so-called 'open systems' approach was not emphasised sufficiently. The commitment of key people in other interdependent units (often middle-level control specialists) must be secured by inviting them to participate in the restructuring studies from the start, and the implications for their work must be considered fully in the analysis. If this is not done they will usually oppose the changes: at best they will not be supportive, and at worst they may use whatever power they have to prevent the new arrangements from working.

In general, socio-technical analysis, in the hands of experts, is a very powerful tool for helping managers to humanise the workplace, partly because it can throw up ways of liberating the employee from some of the tyranny of the technology associated with his work, and partly because it tends to inculcate a healthy habit of looking at what he does in a wider context, and thereby obtaining new insights into its contribution to the business as a whole.

It has become rather a commonplace in company reports for Chairmen to say: 'Our employees are our greatest asset.' This seems a harmless enough statement on the surface, but it is gradually digging itself into our collective corporate subconscious, where it promises to exert a rather unhelpful influence, to say the least.

It seems to the writer that the idea of the employee as an asset — a possession — is at variance with the premises that underlie the humanisation of work. A more useful concept, perhaps, would be that of the employee as a member of his company, accountable for his behaviour (within the limits of his responsibility) in the same sense as his managers. This view is not supported in company law, but it may be that in this respect the law is out of date, as laws often are, and that in any case it is the spirit rather than the letter that matters for our present purpose. Once we can bring ourselves to think of the employee as a user of assets, rather than as an asset himself, we are able to see him in a different light. He becomes at once a responsible person, and as such we must expect him to take his share of responsibility for the prosperity of the enterprise in which he works.

Personnel policies in Shell companies have been changing over the last decade or so in the direction of acknowledging this view of the employee. The accountability of the employee for target-setting, security of information and other things has been increased. Appraisal procedures are joint boss-subordinate affairs, and the employee is expected to share the responsibility for the development of his own career. He is a member of his company, and his managers want to hear his voice. They do not aim to decide for him whether or not he has a problem (though his boss will offer him counsel when he asks for it) and he does not expect to be second-guessed by his managers or by specialist advisers (though he can count on them for support when he needs it). His managers want him to be proud of what he is doing and to think it is worth while making his point when he has one, because at that moment in time his advice, whoever he is, may be the best they can get.

His management is also ready to deal with his representatives, if that is what he prefers. Trades unions and employee councils have been part of the fabric of Shell companies' business for many years and in many different social settings. On balance his managers would rather hear the employee direct, but if it is his wish that he be represented by someone else, or if social conditions so dictate, they are content to have their dialogue with his nominee.

When it comes to the humanisation of work the trades unions are often more reactionary than the managers. Unions have their own problems with politics, bureaucracy and the alienation of their members, and it is perhaps understandable that in many parts of the world they would see collaboration with employers on QWL issues as a potential threat to their traditional power to negotiate wages and conditions of work. The paradoxical elements in this problem will not be removed without a great deal of hard work on both sides, and in some cases it will probably be a long time before mutual trust will be developed to the level at which the employee and the enterprise will begin to reap tangible benefits. We believe, nevertheless, that in the meantime we have to continue to work with the realities of the situation as we perceive them.

This question of perception may be a good one on which to close. We are all workers, after all, in some sense, and perhaps we already have the workplaces we deserve. We tend in our complex modern world to take refuge in stereotypes — the inhuman boss, the lazy worker, the dishonest politician, the trades union agitator, the long-haired OD consultant and the rest. If there are real human beings hidden under those stereotypes struggling to get out they had better hurry up about it, because there is a great deal of work to be done, and not too much time to do it.

References

1. Kelly, J., 'Reflections on the State of the Art', *The Conference Board Record*, Nov. 1975, p. 32.
2. Rogers, C.R., 'The Person of Tomorrow'.
3. Adams, J.W.L., 'Organisation Development', an unpublished paper.

9 DEMOCRATISING THE WORKPLACE
Ernie Roberts

'Hands wanted'. 'Operators wanted'. 'Labour wanted'. Such advertisements for employees by companies show contempt for the feelings and abilities of those who do the useful work in society. They are symptomatic of the attitude of employers to employees, reducing them to the level of 'things for use'. Employees, white- and blue-collar, have combined into trade unions to combat the effects of this attitude, and to gain for themselves a better life in their jobs. To paraphrase Shakespeare, from *The Merchant of Venice*: He who controls the means whereby I live controls my very life.

To free the potential of working people requires that they be given responsibility. The untapped resources of twenty-four million workers constitutes a criminal waste of energy and achievement, as a result of which the majority of workers go through life without even a glimmer of what they could have attained and contributed to their fellow human beings. This is both a personal tragedy and a crime against society. The free expression of each individual's humanity and abilities would promote the well-being and advancement of the whole of society.

Democracy is essential to free human beings. They must have democracy in all aspects of their lives, and above all in the place where they spend a large part of their conscious life: that is, where they learn their livelihood. That applies to the twenty-four million people who do the work in our society, eleven and a quarter million of whom have combined into trade unions, and a further two million have joined professional associations (e.g. British Medical Association), for the purpose of achieving their democratic rights in their jobs. For over a hundred and fifty years, struggles have been fought between trade unionists and employers to establish their rights and to obtain humanised relationships in the workplace.

We have had many defeats, but many victories, too, and these are consolidated in laws on the statute book. Each law represents an armistice in the battle, but the war to humanise our lives goes on. It is fair to say that the victories have been won as a result of combined action by the workers, and the defeats have invariably been in the teeth of strong trade union opposition. Furthermore, the trade union movement has not remained defeated for long: the 1971 Industrial Relations Act, for example, was an unmitigated disaster for both employers and government, simply through the non-cooperation of a large part of the trade-union movement, and 1974 saw the end of this Act and the Industrial Relations Court which was a total failure as regards 'improving' industrial relations.

Recent victories in industrial law have included the Health and Safety Act, the Sex Discrimination Act, and the Employment Protection Act. All worthwhile in their way. But let us not fall into the trap of believing that Humanising the Workplace is a job that can be done entirely by parliamentary means. The Sex Discrimination Act provides 'equal pay for equal work', but nevertheless it took the women engineers at Trico twenty-one weeks to establish and win their case for equal pay. A good law can be a useful aid, but it is not the answer to all industrial problems.

Many workers have lost their health, their limbs, even their lives, in doing their jobs. Sixty years ago, the chances of being killed at work were one in four thousand. Today, the chance is one in fifty thousand. Even so, the last report of the factory inspectorate shows 479 killed and 256,930 injured in industry, in spite of the 1974 Health and Safety at Work Act. Law cannot prevent people from being killed, especially when employers too often put profit before safety. Having won a law, the trade unions have to compel its application.

The new Health and Safety Act provides a basis for protection but it does not do enough. To make the Act effective, the Amalgamated Union of Engineering Workers insists upon the following:

1. The right to make spot-checks between the formal three-monthly inspections.
2. The right of a shop-steward to stop the job where there is risk of serious personal injury.
3. The right of a shop-steward to see HM Inspector before he inspects a workplace.
4. The right to call in advisers of their own choice if necessary.
5. Clarification of the role of Safety Committees.
6. Provision for company- or factory-wide Safety Committees.
7. The right for shop-stewards to interview members in private, following an accident or dangerous occurrence.

In spite of the defects of the Act and the pressure upon them to extend its provisions, the Government has not made financial resources available for the provision of safety representatives and the setting up of safety committees in the 1977 session of Parliament.

Health and safety are two aspects of industrial democracy which cannot and must not be left to management. Workers must always insist — both out of consideration for their fellow workers and out of self-interest — that methods of production and the products themselves are in no way dangerous to the health and well-being of humans. The use of toxic materials should be outlawed — for example, cadmium, chrome and other chemicals and liquid coolants used in industry which produce cancer and other forms of human poisoning.

Employees should not be expected to risk life and limb in the interests of profit. We know that the piecework system of payment causes many workers to take unnecessary risks on the job. Piecework is an anti-social method of determining wage-levels. All workers should have proper pay levels based on their usefulness to society and not on their sweat.

Like the law on Health and Safety, the Sex Discrimination Act is only a new, slightly higher step from which to carry on the struggle. In spite of the Act, the women engineering workers at Trico had to strike for over five months during 1976 to win equal pay with men for the same work. But equal pay is not the whole problem: for women to gain the same rights and dignity in their jobs they must not only have the same pay, but also equal opportunity to advance in their careers. This means equal training opportunity for women on any job that a man does.

The Sex Discrimination Act will not solve this problem. Women themselves must be convinced of their equality, and be prepared to use their organised strength to convince others that they are, or can become, the equals of any man. It is in the men's interests to fight with the women for equality, too, in order to avoid the situation of women being used as 'cheap hands' to undercut the men's rate.

The job of an engineering technician can be a challenging one, including design, marketing, manufacturing processes, estimating, costing, purchasing, and a wide range of other aspects of engineering. In order to encourage girls into engineering, the Engineering Industry Training Board offers fifty scholarships annually to school-leavers for a period of two years, starting with 1976. A praiseworthy effort, no doubt. But we should bear in mind that the number of girls in the engineering industry alone who get little or no training can be counted in thousands, and a mere fifty scholarships is a drop in the ocean of their job dissatisfaction. We must humanise the workplace by removing all sex prejudice, and this must start in the schools, for it is at school-age that women are programmed to become something less than men, who themselves are something less than human in some of the jobs they are compelled to do.

The training problem, therefore, is two-fold; first, to increase the overall availability of training, both on and off the job, to ensure that training is offered to all who want it; second, to ensure an adequate proportion of that training goes to girls, who are more likely than ever before to keep their jobs and extend their careers beyond marriage. One of the most inhuman aspects of factory-work, in particular, has been the encouragement of a conveyor-belt mentality — an acceptance of a small part of a job (tightening screws, or putting on a wheel or a door, for example) without seeing its relationship to the job as a whole. This Adam Smith concept is as outdated as *The Wealth of Nations*, and training schemes must include broader involvement in and wider knowledge of the processes of production.

One problem which has led in the past to dictatorship in the workplace is the problem of 'managerial rights and functions', which may be interpreted as 'the right of the employer to do what he likes with his own' — including his employees. The trade unions, especially in the engineering industries, have always fought against this, and it has led to many strikes. In 1922, the employers introduced the 'York Memorandum' for dealing with disputes, and this procedure was based on the 'managerial rights' philosophy. Fifty years later, in 1972, the Engineering Trade Unions gave notice that the York Memorandum was to cease, and there was a three-year-long battle to establish a new procedure, which is more democratic: it does not take so long to get a decision, and — most important — 'managerial dictatorship' has been curtailed. A 'status quo' clause in the new Agreement states:

> It is agreed that in the event of any difference arising which cannot be immediately disposed of, then whatever practice or agreement existed prior to the difference shall continue to operate pending a settlement or until the agreed procedure has been exhausted.

This is a most basic and elementary principle of democracy; yet management has had to *learn* to act democratically, and to discuss problems with the worker or his representative on the job, instead of making unilateral decisions. No longer can he say, 'Yours is not to reason why, yours is just to do or die.'

This sort of industrial democracy is basic to humanising the workplace. Employees are no longer 'hands', 'operators' or 'labour' — they insist upon being treated as human beings, with equal rights with all other humans. How far democracy should be allowed to proceed is, however, a matter of some concern to management, who do not relinquish their privileges without a struggle.

The following excerpts from a statement by one Mr Appleby, a business executive, in the Magazine *Production Engineer* are an example of the difficulties faced by the workers:

> One of the underlying assumptions concerning industrial democracy is that the organs of the managerial apparatus should include representatives of the people doing the work and that this should take place at all levels of management in the enterprise. It is necessary to question this concept. . . . In my view any involvement on the part of the people doing the work in the decision-making process ought to be based upon competence and experience rather than on representation . . . I do not regard the representative system as being a very practical one. Theoretically it is part of the democratic process in that the representative would normally be elected by ballot. Practically, however, and as in the trade union movement or stockholders' meetings, the elected representatives can gain office from a very limited percentage of the franchise.

Mr Appleby has himself answered both his objections. Of course the decision-making process should be carried out by competent and experienced people. And who is more experienced or more competent than the person on the job? Workers would be elected into the decision-making process because of those very qualities, by their work-mates. There is no special advantage, and more likely many disadvantages, in choosing an outsider to take decisions on behalf of the workers. Far better to elect somebody who has learnt his job and knows what is involved in it. As regards the 'limited franchise', Mr Appleby must surely be joking! At least in a shop-floor ballot, everybody would have the opportunity to vote, even if some of them turned down the chance. But the decision of a board of directors to appoint someone to office is a 'limited franchise' *par excellence*!

Another red herring often introduced under the guise of 'employee involvement' is the idea of co-partnership. Hidden among a mass of suggestions on how to improve the workers' lot without actually conceding anything to them, there are two or three useful proposals. Nigel Vinson, Chairman of the Industrial Co-partnership Association, mentioned (in a conference on the subject of involvement) the importance of job enrichment — for example, assembling a complete product, not merely a part of it, so that the worker feels some sense of pride in the result.

But the few useful ideas are wrapped up in a welter of padding: ways of giving workers the illusion of being involved. Mr Vinson talks about 'diminishing the phoney class barriers' between office and works, by having common canteen facilities, common toilets, the same car park for staff and works, and air-conditioning in works offices as well as staff offices. These are all pleasant though very minor ways of humanising the workplace. Such suggestions sound so patronising as to be almost offensive, and in any case there should never be any question about common facilities for all workers. So much for diminishing the 'phoney' class barriers! When it comes to dealing with the *real* class barriers, the co-partnership scheme begins to show its true colours: people at work should always be told what is going on, says Mr Vinson, but a truly humanised workplace would *ask* employees what to do — or how it should be done — not tell them. After all, the combined intelligence, experience and skill of the workers in any company is greater than that of any individual Managing Director, or Board of Directors. The problem is one of organising that intelligence in the interests of the people, and that can only be done through genuine industrial democracy — the sort of industrial democracy experienced to a degree during the 1939-45 war when workers were allowed to have a say in production and distribution.

If co-partnership were intended to be really democratic, it would, instead of giving a worker a holiday on his birthday and offering him legal advice (which he can get from his union anyway!), direct itself towards more basic needs of workers in industry: towards mechanisation of humdrum jobs, for example, with a consequent reduction in working hours without loss of pay. Employers often seem to lose sight of the fact that industries and services were created to serve human beings and not vice versa. In the future, it should become increasingly practicable to arrange hours of work to suit employees, and to operate flexi-time systems, so that the jobs suit the people, instead of people constantly arranging their lives to suit the jobs. These considerations should be the *right* of the workers, not a bonus patronisingly offered by management, which is all that co-partnership amounts to.

The workers' representative on the job is generally the shop steward, who until recently has usually operated in conditions which might have been specially designed to hamper him in his job as workers' spokesman.

Democratising the Workplace

The Commission on Industrial Relations made some proposals for improving facilities for shop stewards, but my own demands — which I had been publicly advocating for some time before the CIR made its report — would give shop stewards a far better chance of carrying out their functions properly than the recommendations of the CIR. My proposals are:

1. Election of shop stewards to be the prerogative of the trade unions, with no interference whatsoever from the employer.
2. The employer to provide all necessary facilities for the election of shop stewards.
3. The shop stewards to represent all workpeople in the department.
4. Recognition of convenors.
5. Facilities for convenors: office, office services, telephone, duplicating machinery, etc.
6. Payment by management to shop stewards for all time lost on trade union business within the company.
7. The right of trade unions to choose their own side when discussions are taking place at plant level.
8. The setting-up of shop stewards' committees.
9. Facilities for reporting-back by delegates the proceedings of any discussions concerning the plant.
10. The setting-up of safety committees, with facilities for the election of trade union representatives on such committees.
11. Shop stewards' representation on apprentice committees.
12. Facilities for shop stewards to interview all employees prior to engagement.
13. No worker to be dismissed without his shop steward being consulted.
14. No shop steward to be dismissed or suspended without discussion with the trade union.
15. The status quo to apply while a dispute is going through procedure.
16. The right of shop stewards to examine all books and records of the firm and to be given any information required about the company.

With these principles established, the liaison between worker and management via the union would be ensured.

In talking of management, we must make a distinction between the management of private industry and the management of nationalised industries. So far, the distinction has made very little practical difference to the workers, but in future we must make sure that the control by workers over the management of nationalised industries is extended as far as possible. Two of the proposals made by my own union, the Amalgamated Union of Engineering Workers (Engineering Section), to the Bullock Commission on Industrial Democracy, make clear this distinction; on private industry, they say: 'In the private sector we should proceed towards industrial democracy through an unlimited extension of collective bargaining.' The recommendation on nationalised industries is much more far-reaching: 'In the nationalised industries we should become involved in decision-making, seeking majority trade union representation at board level and effective controls at other levels.'

It is a sad fact of life that, as regards workers' control, the nationalised industries have no better a record than private industries. Many workers hoped for better things following the nationalisation of British Leyland, but in fact the new management structure at Leyland excludes workers from real power, asserts managerial rights, and requires workers' representatives to be subservient to management. This is not the industrial democracy that the trade unions through the TUC and the Labour Party Conference have been fighting for.

We trade unionists must get the principles of workers' control clear in our minds:

- direct election of all representatives to all levels of management including the corporate management board in all nationalised industries and services
- representation of trade unionists in the wider movement (TUC and Trades Councils) and from local authorities
- trade unions to have a majority on the board
- such industries and services to be responsible to a minister and answerable to Parliament
- all workers' representatives to be subject to recall by their electorate
- all representatives to report back to their constituencies, which must be small enough to permit discussion and decision
- boards at all levels of nationalised industries and services must select and control all technical and administrative management personnel
- the whole process of trade union collective bargaining on wages

and conditions must be separated from trade union representatives on the board and remain in the hands of trade union representatives, e.g. shop stewards, District Committees and full-time officials.

This method of representation by direct election would give employees a sense of ownership and personal responsibility towards their industry. There would be constant involvement in the decision-making process through consultation. The interest arising from knowledge about the employee's own job would be maintained and augmented by giving employees the opportunity to change from one job to another, to see their job as part of the whole process, or to take part in poly-technical development such as the groupwork at Alfred Herbert, or at Volvo in Sweden, where small groups of workers see the job through from start to finish.

'Humanising the workplace' could in such circumstances cover a multitude of concepts, from basic principles (e.g. the right to talk to other workers on the job where this is practicable), through the right to determine personal working conditions (e.g. establishing agreed scales of pay, with few variations and small gaps between grades; determining collectively the rate at which a new entrant should start on the job), and on to the principles of production — what to produce, how to produce it, and the quality and quantity to be produced.

Workers are not only capable of making all these decisions, they are also in many cases far better equipped to make them than managers and directors are, having experience on the job to back up their decisions. Boards of directors represent the interests of shareholders, who only invest money in industry, while the workers invest their lives in their jobs. So if the workplace is to be humanised, the worker must take more control over 'the means whereby he lives', and therefore over his life.

10 THE STATE OF THE UNIONS
Mick Rice

Introduction

The purpose of this chapter is to examine the way that trade unions operate and to discover from their practice where they fall down. Inevitably we will need to suggest ways for improving and extending the role of the unions for it can only be by organised workers that industry can be democratically controlled and the democratic control of industry cannot be separated from the democratic control of society. Two of the factors which we will consider are the structures of the unions and the nature of the work process itself. The trade unions have played a significant role in beginning the humanisation of the work process, but they are caught in a dilemma, for they deal with the effects and not with the cause. They see their role as challenging managerial authority within the confines of accepting the control of the economic system.

Division of labour is natural

The division of labour has existed from the earliest societies, indeed the division of labour is almost synonymous with the term society. Even primitive man organised his existence so that those most suitable for hunting, for example, became the hunters. This division occurred in a natural way in that those people with certain natural talents and attributes undertook specific tasks for the benefit of the community.

In primitive societies the goal of the community was to maintain its physical existence against the ravages of nature in a life or death struggle. Furthermore this goal was shared equally by all members of the society for they all had a stake in defending their own lives, which maintained the existence of their society. The rationale for society was simply that the total wealth generated was greater than that which individuals could produce fending for themselves. The creation of society was therefore a form of self-protection, since the individual could, through society, increase his chance of survival. This concept of society was not worked out in any contractual way, for 'individual man' did not sit down and come to an arrangement with his fellows. Nor for that matter did 'individual man' exist except in the temporary situation where a man was expelled from society and that meant death. The point is that society became established because it provided a superior form of production. We would expect therefore that as society developed, man's control over nature would increase. While society began in order to ensure man's existence no one yet can claim that the continued existence of man is guaranteed.

As society has become more sophisticated the stark reality of a life or death struggle with nature has receded. The very sophistication of society has removed it from the control of its members. It is not therefore the division of labour which has dehumanised society and the work process, rather it is that the development of society has changed the method by which this division is decided. The goal of society is no longer collectively determined. The division of labour has become ever more specialised, so much so that individual products are broken down into component parts. There are very few instances left in modern society where an individual worker produces commodities for the market. Commodities are produced by collective labour involved in a collective production process. This method of production is the norm and has reached its highest form in the modern factory.

Fragmentation in the workplace

The location of work in factory units has created fragmentation. Workers feel that their product has no value and only becomes of worth when assembled together into the final commodity. But they have recognised that the products of their labour are inextricably bound together and that therefore their individual interests as workers are inextricably bound up with the interests of their fellow workers. But this awareness is mediated by a whole host of factors and only rarely gives rise to complete working class consciousness. Workers often see the concreteness of their unity and organisation in terms of unity amongst their fellow tradesmen. That means that their unity is on the basis of skill similarities, on the basis of working for the same establishment, working for the same company, or working in the same industry.

The trade unions are the first organisational expressions of the desire of workers to reintegrate society into line with their needs. In order to assert some measure of control over their working environment workers have created collective organisations. These organisations were formed because of a limited collective consciousness and awareness imparted by the productive process itself. Individually workers have no voice over their rates and conditions. They are powerless. Collectively they have forced managements to see that labour is not some passive element in the productive process. The unions have made managements listen to the problems of workers and to go some way towards resolving those problems.

A second fragmentation in the workplace is the development of the unions into national institutions. This happened because union leaders saw the need for the creation of national organisations. Some of the pioneers saw that the long term viability of geographically based unions would be hazardous, especially where local employers could combine and go on an offensive against the union. In some cases the mobility of the membership has spurred on this process. The old Amalgamated Society of Engineers, formed in 1851, laid down within its rules the provision that local branches should provide for its members on the tramp around the country in search of work.

Whilst the role of the national unions is valuable, the horizons of the membership is often far more limited. So much so that the unions can be analysed more satisfactorily if we see the unions as collections of members organised in separate parts. The most intense awareness of the workers' collective consciousness is with his mates. This intensity lessens as union activity gets further removed from the work mates. Combined shop stewards committees are an effort to extend this intensity to a company basis.

Trade unions in Britain have developed organically. The major impetus for their growth has been the growth of British Industry, so their growth has not been linear, nor clear cut. Industrial relations writers generally identify three ideal types of union organisations: craft unions, industrial unions and general unions. As their names imply craft unions recruit on the basis of common skills, industrial unions recruit people within a particular industry, and general unions can recruit anybody. Although it is possible to categorise the majority of unions under one of these three headings, in practice they tend to have shared characteristics.

Historically the craft and industrial unions were established first. The general unions were established after 1889 but only became important after the amalgamations of the early 1920s. As a consequence of this uneven development, today workers find themselves confronted with a multiplicity of unions. This is particularly the case in the engineering industry and an example of a third fragmentation in the workplace.

In my factory there are four unions covering the manual workers. These are the AUEW (engineering section) whose roots stem from a

The State of the Unions

craft organisation. They organise the skilled workers and a large proportion of the general workforce. The T&GWU organises the rest of the general workforce. The NUSMWCH&DE, which is a craft union, organises the sheetmetal workers, and the EEPTU which has also had a craft background and in this instance a craft practice, for they are confined to the electricians.

The members and the shop stewards in our various unions have a good and fraternal relationship, but all of us are bound by the constitutions of our separate organisations. Whenever any major questions arise we have to take notice of the separate policies of our respective unions.

Superimposed on these differences, due to the workforce's membership in different unions, are the differences which arise from the existence of various trade group negotiating committees. The toolmakers, for example, negotiate their rates and conditions through a combined shop stewards' group from all of the other company factories within the area. This trade group negotiating structure applies to the electricians, the toolsetters and the works engineering department.

A number of shop stewards' committees within the company have also set up a Combine Shop Stewards organisation which attempts to cover all of the membership, both manual and staff, within the company. This organisation has no negotiating rights as such but attempts to liaise between the various unions and sites at a rank and file level on the basis of making recommendations.

The loyalty of the workforce is therefore divided by their membership of the different unions and by their attachment to various skilled negotiating groups. The Combine organisation on the other hand attempts to develop the maximum unity between the workers on the basis of the common employer. In the future we might expect more shop stewards in particular factories, areas, and industries to combine themselves into committees. Combine committees will tend to overcome much of the fragmentation of union efforts in an already fragmented workplace.

Today's workplace

As an active trades unionist working in the engineering industry, I am continually confronted with a work situation where the nature of the work itself, or at least the way that it is presently organised, and the attitudes that derive from it, create and foster divisions amongst the workforce.

Indirect workers are those paid for hours clocked rather than pieces of work completed. They, for example, do not have to do repetitive work on the same machine all day. The tempo is less than that of the direct production worker who has to justify his hours by the total units produced at the end of the shift.

The indirect worker, therefore, has more time to chat to his mates than the production worker, and the more chats and discussions that take place, the greater the work group cohesion and solidarity. This difference in work content influences the union awareness and involvement of the workers.

The shop steward of indirect workers can in many instances spend much of his time talking to his members, for his work is only required when a machine breaks down or when the supply of components dries up. In contrast to this, assembly line workers complain if the steward is off the job for long because they are paid on a team basis. When the steward is off the job the remaining workers have to cover for him and they consequently earn less money.

The apprentice system and the skilled status of a section of the workforce reinforces the tendency within these grades for the indirect workers to be more cohesive and more involved in the affairs of the union. For example, traditionally, skilled workers have been extremely concerned over the question of dilution. From their point of view, and correctly so, they see the union's task as controlling the number of workers admitted to the trade. By limiting the intake and through demanding proper training they have been able to ensure better conditions and a differential over the rest of the manual workforce.

But this situation does create the conditions where skilled workers sometimes view themselves as a privileged elite and the rest of the workforce are regarded as Tom Nods. This is a toolmakers term which is used in my area of the country. The origin of this term and its precise definition is unclear, but it means, in effect, that the rest of the workforce are one step removed from monkeys.

But while the skilled status of a section of the workforce can lead to craft bigotry it can also have positive features. The knowledge that a worker is doing a job involving skill lifts the spirit, makes the worker more fulfilled and leads to an independence in outlook. Often the really skilled worker is regarded as his own man because of this independence. In this instance supervision cannot tell the worker what he must do — they have to discuss the job or seek advice on the best way of dealing with the problem.

The craft divisions existing between manual workers, while still very strong, have broken down considerably in the post-war period. This has been primarily due to full employment which has led to the creation of joint shop stewards' committees. Joint union organisation covering all trades necessarily means that workers see their identity of interests in relation to the employer. We see, therefore, that the creation and extension of joint shop stewards' committees is the organisational expression of a change in workers attitudes, both towards themselves and to their fellow workers, caused by a change in economic conditions. But even where this state of affairs exists skilled workers are nearly always more dominant in the union structure and in the factory than their numerical strength warrants. The reason for this is that skilled men are tradesmen. Tradesmen generally undertake the same job for the whole of their working lives and this means that they will stay in the same industry. In addition they will remain in the same union. It is likely, therefore, that the skilled worker will at some point during his life become involved in the union in an active way. Awareness of union procedure and union terminology is generally higher amongst skilled workers than amongst semi and unskilled workers. Production workers may have had other jobs outside of the industry. A number will have had skilled jobs but have lost them through the development of automation or the decline of their old industry. Because some indirect workers provide a service for the whole of the factory they are economically more powerful than direct workers. When indirect workers take action the whole of the factory is affected. Negotiating procedures often take account of this and the representatives of skilled sections (indirect) have immediate access to factory management to present their claims. From all of this, it is virtually inevitable that skilled workers play a role in union structure which is in general out of proportion to their numerical strength.

This example of the difference between skilled and other workers takes on another dimension in that opportunities for skill training are not uniformly available. Sexual and racial differences built into society mean that women and black workers have less chance to become skilled. Certainly in the large engineering establishments in my vicinity, as the nature of the job becomes more skilled the proportion of women and blacks in those jobs diminishes.

We see therefore that whilst unions have relatively democratic structures with the members having equal rights, the nature of the work process and society itself means that those rights are exercised more consistently by some sections of the membership than by others. The varying and sometimes competing loyalties of union members can be traded on by the factory trade union leadership. In fact any union leader with experience is always weighing carefully the state and level of his union in relation to the tasks which he believes ought to be carried out.

The unions have proved successful at a micro level. In the workshops and offices management do not have absolute control. Their control is limited by the existence of union organisation. Continually management have found their decisions challenged, which has caused decisions to be revised. A permanent feature of present management thinking is the estimation of the response from the workforce to any new initiative. This is so common nowadays that a further and more refined stage is being actively promoted by managements. They are beginning to say, if only workers were involved at the outset, or so the thinking goes, in arriving at decisions then they would understand the need for these decisions to be acted upon. If only workers shared the same pressures as management then they would understand the importance of adhering to new workloads and working arrangements.

It is precisely at this stage that unions fall down. In Britain, unlike other European countries, the unions were formed organically in response to the development of industry. In other countries religious or political considerations have limited the boundaries of union growth, but in Britain union membership has never meant that the members should have any fundamental ideological commitment to a new society. In part of course this has helped the unions to grow for it takes care of objections from potential members whose political ideas are hostile to the extension of workers power in the political arena. Significantly these problems are 'resolved' not by means of argument or the presentation of alternative ideas for controlling the productive process, but by ignoring these questions.

Unions and politics

The unions then appeal to the class position of workers and demonstrate their effectiveness and worth in relation to the foreman and factory manager, but they studiously avoid any coherent theory of their role in changing the economic basis of society. This question is a political one and the unions separate the industrial struggle from the political struggle. Politics is seen as something outside of the productive process. Politics is seen as something to do with winning electoral support for the Labour Party in local and parliamentary elections.

But this separation only applies to the rank and file members. The national union officials, by virtue of the immense power they can potentially exercise, are integrated into the political process by the system of the block vote at Labour Party Conferences. Union leaders have different priorities from their members for their position and respect stems from the fact that they straddle both the desires of their members and the existing status quo. The function of union leaders is to do a deal between two sides, they therefore have a dual responsibility in maintaining the two sides in existence. The safety valve for the existing establishment lies in the ability of the union leaders to direct the struggle of their members away from clear confrontation which could undermine the stability of the state.

Factory union leaders are therefore faced with immense problems since they only possess influence directly over partial organisations. If we take an actual example we can see what this means. In a redundancy situation the policy that shop stewards attempt to get their members to adopt is generally along the following lines:

1. No mobility of members. That is no coverage of jobs when jobs are in jeopardy.
2. No overtime working. No worker should do more than fulfill his contractual obligations for by so doing he destroys the possibility of maintaining those jobs which are in jeopardy.
3. For sharing the available work amongst the existing workforce.

But these policies, whilst they place difficulties in the path of management, do not go anywhere near resolving the redundancy problem. The level of employment depends upon the economic policies of the Government. Governments can and do alter the amount of money in circulation which thereby effects the total demand for products. Redundancy does not happen in isolation from the rest of society. It therefore cannot be dealt with on a partial basis.

Nationalisation and the workers

After the war union members saw the solution to their problems through government legislation. The nationalisation of some of the basic industries, the introduction of the health and education acts must have channelled the activities of many active trade unionists away from the factory and towards the local Labour Party wards. But whilst these people saw nationalisation as something which would begin the process of changing the social basis of society, they have been proved wrong.

Strange as it may seem in these days of full-blooded *laissez-faire* Toryism, the Conservatives were the first party to introduce nationalisation when the British Overseas Airways Corporation was set up in the

1930s. Oliver Stanley, a Tory who was President of the Board of Trade, even introduced a bill to nationalise coal royalties. The nationalisation of the basic industries was carried out for far more pragmatic reasons than to extend the power of workers in society. Many businessmen realised that some of the basic industries could only be run on an efficient basis through national control and planning. Nationalisation was the only way to achieve this is a short space of time. A good example of this was the pressure from businessmen to nationalise the railways so their goods would not be lost between lines or charged for transferring. The practice of nationalisation soon impinged upon the illusions of some of the workers. On at least one occasion the *élan* of the workers on the nationalisation of their industry turned into a backlash. As the *Economist* (1947) stated on the strike at Grimethorpe colliery a few months after nationalisation:

> The real issue which is being fought out at Grimethorpe, where the miners have now been on strike for more than three weeks, can be summed up as a struggle between nationalisation and syndicalism. The argument over the extra working at the coal face appears to be merely the pretext for a show-down on whether control is to be exercised by an all-powerful Board or whether the workers are to be given a measure of influence in the management of their own pits. Many miners expected nationalisation to result in workers' control; instead it has resulted in a large bureaucratic machine leaving the individual miner face to face with the same managers with whom he has been wrangling over the past twenty years.
> This is an issue on which the National Coal Board cannot be defeated, for management and responsibility cannot be divorced. Managers must manage, and there is no reserve of experienced colliery managers on whom the Board can draw to replace those who are already there. Only time can solve this problem — time to educate already existing staff and to train new men in modern mining techniques and in staff management; time to convince the miners that the past is really done away with. But, as Mr Morrison said, it is time that is the greatest shortage. In the Grimethorpe case all the official negotiations were conducted correctly: full agreement was reached between the local officials of the Board and the union; the extra stint was considered feasible. But the men have rebelled; they refuse to use the conciliation machinery or to accept the offices of the more remote union representatives. There appears to be no other explanation than that they wish to decide the issue themselves;

hence the spread of sympathetic strikes around them.

Tom Mann, over forty years before, when he was the main British exponent of Industrial Syndicalism had the following to say about nationalisation:

> The Industrial Syndicalist declares that to run industry through Parliament, i.e. by state machinery, will be even more mischievous to the working class than the existing method, for it will assuredly mean that the capitalist class will, through government departments, exercise over the natural forces, and over the workers, a domination even more rigid than is the case today.

One would find it extremely difficult to disagree with him in light of the shrinkage of labour, the introduction of managerial techniques and the general low pay enjoyed by public workers since the war.

One can now see that nationalisation does not increase the power or the control of the worker over his immediate work environment. We can also question whether nationalisation increases his power in society in general. In reality nationalisation is State control and the issue then is who controls the State. At the moment in our society this does not mean that workers have any additional rights.

Decline of shop stewards' bargaining role

During the boom period after the second world war power in the unions became decentralised for shop stewards and their committees could in many instances win concessions from management which satisfied the aspirations of the membership. During this period the new phenomenon of wage drift appeared. Wage drift is the difference between actual earnings and nationally negotiated rates of pay. The employers found their bargaining position diminishing because of labour shortage and the seemingly permanent quasi-boom conditions allowed companies to pass increases on to the public.

Comparability, always a cardinal principle in determining the outlook of trade unionists, became accentuated. Inter-industry comparisons became intra-industry, intra-company and even intra-department as wage relativities changed. Different shop stewards' committees and different shop stewards vied with one another to achieve the best rates and conditions.

The mechanism which gave shop stewards so much power in the engineering and allied trades and which built up their confidence was piecework bargaining. This had taken between thirty and forty years to introduce in the late nineteenth and early twentieth century and had been bitterly opposed by the trade unions at the time. They correctly saw it as an attempt to increase competition amongst the workers. In fact its introduction gave rise to the shop stewards' movement when one man would come to be regarded as the most skillful negotiator and his mates would ask him to look after their interests.

The piecework system though had inherently built within it a rachet mechanism — for workers would always put up resistance to new rates that meant cuts in wages. At a time when there were long runs of standard jobs and change was not rapid this might have been acceptable, but with full employment and regularly changing product specifications, over a period of years significant increases could be made in wages. The demand for parity and the maintenance of differentials multiplied this upward movement in industries where piecework applied.

The influence and power of the shop stewards increased at their ability to gain marked improvements in wages and conditions. With this power their confidence increased and they upped their demands and raised their objectives even higher. For many union members the remoteness of their officials made no difference as they had the necessary strength within the factory to gain what they were seeking.

Essentially the whole period since the sixties has been characterised by attempts to hold in check wage increases (or to extract more for more) and all the new 'scientific managerial techniques' and the industrial and economic policies of successive governments has been designed with this end in view.

Managements therefore have tried to do the following things:

1. Abolish piecework and introduce new incentive schemes which did not give the same opportunity for renegotiation. Measured day work, which is extremely complex and costly to introduce, has in significant areas of industry replaced piecework.
2. Introduce long-term agreements which allow companies to budget for wage costs and which further diminishes the ability for renegotiation.
3. Categorise workers into different grades so as to reduce demands for differential pay awards.
4. Change the principle for negotiations so that it is accepted *a priori* that increases can only be paid out of increased productivity.

The State of the Unions

5. Remove negotiation from the shop floor to the trade union official.

Even if all of these conditions apply to a particular company the problems are not completely solved, for external influences can destroy stability. The Ford strike in 1971 is a case in point for in the company all of the above conditions applied but a claim for parity with outside firms doing similar work provided the rationale for a nine week strike and led to a substantial pay increase. The success which managements have had in introducing the measures outlined above has led to the partial breakdown of sectionalised bargaining and the deepening economic crisis has meant that managements have not been able to yield to the claims of their workforces.

Successive governments have increased their intervention in collective bargaining since the early sixties. Essentially their policies are variations around two main strategies: incomes policy and industrial legislation. Other government policies are more directly economic and include changes in the tax structure, devaluation and deflationary policies. All of these policies are designed to restore the profitability of British Industry.

Incomes policy and industrial legislation, the two policies which directly impinge on collective bargaining appear to follow a cyclical pattern because the effectiveness of any particular policy is only temporary. Incomes policy began in 1961 when Selwyn Lloyd introduced a pay pause (incomes policy has been used before in the late forties). In 1965 a voluntary incomes policy was agreed with the trade union leaders. In 1966 there was a statutory wage control followed by a period of severe restraint. Eventually the Labour Government attempted to introduce legislation, the ill-fated 'In place of strife', to change the whole basis of industrial relations. The following Conservative government introduced the Industrial Relations Act, whilst at the same time continuing with a limited form of incomes policy by attempting to reduce the settlements to their own employees by at least one per cent less than the previous settlement. They then introduced statutory controls on wages with the Counter Inflation Act. The Labour Government likewise, after the second election of 1974, introduced controls on wages and these have continued to the present time. It is this interference in the affairs of grass roots trade unionsim that is slowly having an impact. The role of unions as a whole, and therefore their national leadership, has become far more important than ten or fifteen years ago. Pressures developing at the base of the trade unions has seen the growth and extension of lay member organisations such as Combine Committees and industry wide national committees of shop stewards. These activities are clearly separate from the official structures. Factory union leaders are beginning to extend their partial organisation and are taking in workers from all unions within their industry or company. The fragmentation of union organisation is no longer viable. In the coming period union members will increase the pressure for the establishment of industry-wide unions. The motive force for these changes is the struggle of workers to maintain their living standards. Combined with this breaking down of union fragmentation will be an increasing political awareness.

Conclusion

The wage-labour relationship is the economic expression of the difference between the worker and the employer. Workers are employed to produce a surplus but workers undertake employment for money. They are the opposite ends of the same equation and the attitude of a person to the work process is fundamentally determined by their standpoint on one or other side of the human equation. The worker by the very fact that his identification has to be paid for with money is therefore really alienated from the work process. His real thoughts and involvement lie elsewhere. He has to be bribed to give up his time. This means that as long as work is performed for money then the process will remain inhuman.

Obviously, before this statement is misunderstood, this does not entail a reactionary call for a return to a slave-based work process. Instead, when people work for the joy of it then the process will be truly human. Now this idea may be startling for people whose whole training and experience in society has taught them that the value of work can only be measured in terms of financial reward. So ingrained is this notion that many people will undoubtedly refuse to give the idea serious thought and dismiss it as a utopian dream.

This would be unfortunate for it is probably generally recognised that intense pleasure is gained by many people who work for their own enjoyment and without the intention to gain financial reward. The fact that people are prepared to and do use up a lot of energy in pursuit of an interest which is pleasurable demonstrates that people are not inherently lazy. The natural state of man is not just consuming the products of others labour. Man's final goal is not just the passive consumption of the necessary goods for life support. For it also consists of the pleasure of production. The distinction between leisure and work has to be broken down for the productive process to become more human.

Technological advance has always meant that man's labour becomes less necessary for the production of economic goods. Machines increasingly reduce the number of work hours needed to produce goods to satisfy basic human requirements.

A future age of affluence releases man from the struggle to maintain his existence in the face of the ravages of nature. When that battle is won, when the economic necessities are freely available, a choice presents itself. To work when it is no longer necessary is truly creative and human.

Whilst the long term trend is the elimination of the need for work, until this is economically possible transitional stages of society will be necessary. When the economic crisis of society has demonstrated its inability to provide the basic requirements for life, then the unions, reinvigorated by the active involvement and politicisation of their members, will be able to begin the task of making society, once again, responsible to man. The humanisation of work can only begin when collective organisation involving all those who produce decide the priorities. The goal of society will then be collectively determined and shared.

References

'The Issue at Grimethorpe', *Economist*, Vol CLIII, No. 5428, 6 Sept. 1947, p. 393.

INDEX

absenteeism 65
American 17
alienation 102, 118, 137ff
apprentice system 162
apology 13
attitudes 139ff
autonomy 47, 50, 57, 58, 62

banking method 86, 92
Brazil 78
bureaucratic organisations 46, 57, 58

capitalist 29
capital (fixed) 66
cathect 103
centralisation 47, 48, 58
change 13; agents 95; committment to 139; organisational 14, 22, 130; structural 45
circles of culture 94, 95, 98
class system 82, 83
collusion 21
competition 39
computer/operator interface 59, 60
computer technology 44, 45, 50, 52, 58, 61, 62
computer systems 44
conscientization 84, 88, 90
consciousness: semi- 85; naive 85; full 85
control systems 47, 48, 50, 58
co-ordinator 95, 98
cultural factors 19

decentralisation 58, 59, 61
decision-making 49, 58, 125, 137
democracy 149
discovery/push 31

economics (economy) of scale 38ff, 144
education for workers 80, 126
educational system 131
effectiveness 142
ego states: 102ff; adult 102ff; child 102ff; contaminated 102ff; exclusive 102ff; parent 102ff

encounter groups 21

factory 27, 28, 38, 66
fatigue 70
feedback 46
flexibility 47, 52, 59, 61, 63, 140
fragmentation 159

Health and Safety Act 150
hierarchical organisations 123
humanising the workplace 13, 25, 29, 30, 43, 138, 152, 157

incomes policy 169
industrial democracy 91ff, 152
information 46, 48, 49, 50, 59, 61
integration 46
inventions 26, 31

job content 46, 49, 52

Labour Party 164
laws 149
learning 15
literacy programmes 89
Little Professor 102

management: 160; education 81; objectives 54, 58, 59, 61; participation 123; role 124
managers 136, 143ff
man/machine interaction 70
Marx 29
matrix working 145

nationalisation 165
need/push 32
neutrality 52, 58
non-hierarchical systems 58, 59, 60, 62

oppressed groups 80
oppression 83ff
organisation: culture 139; development 136, 137, 138; structures 46, 57, 58; characteristics 45

172

Index

passivity 116
perspective: psychological 81; sociological 80
philosophy 56, 57
piece work 168
power élites 85
problem-posing method 87, 88
push/pull 32
quality of work life 136, 141

rational 20
responsibility for education 127

scientific management 71, 142
scripts 110
Sex Discrimination Act 150
shop stewards 98, 155, 161, 162
small is beautiful 42
social scientists 101
social skills 128
social responsibility 139, 141
specialisation 45, 46, 59
strokes 108ff; deprivation 112
supervisors 47, 51
symbiosis 113; chain 115; mutual 115
synchronised computers 69
systems designers 53, 54, 56, 57, 58, 62, 63

tasks 45, 61
technological: Darwinism 26, 27; determinism 25, 26, 27, 29, 30, 42, 53, 145; change 25, 30; cycles 35; innovation 31; paradigm 37
Third World 79
T-Group 79, 94, 95, 96, 97, 98, 99
trade unions 56, 147, 156, 159ff
Transactional Analysis 101ff
transactions 105ff

values 53, 54, 63, 136

Women's Movement 90, 91
workers: education 78ff; indirect 161; manual 160; views 78

yalks 72
York memorandum 152

AUTHOR INDEX

Adams, J.W.L. 138
Argyris, C. 79, 113, 114

Babbage, C. 72
Bamforth, R. 15
Beckhard, R. 130
Benne, K.D. 79, 94
Bennis, W. 56
Berger, B. 86
Berger, M. 128
Berger, P.L. 80, 86
Berne, E. 108, 109, 119
Bernholz, A. 70
Blake, R.R. 113, 131
Bradford, L.P. 79, 81, 94
Braverman, H. 76
Brown, M. 106
Buckingham, W.S. 28
Butler, D. 82
Burns, T. 45

Cherns, A. 53, 129
Coch, L. 15, 16
Cooley, M.J.E. 67, 70, 73
Cooper, C.L. 125, 128
Crozier, M. 45

Darendorf, R. 82
Davis, L.E. 129, 132
Dickson, D. 26, 68

Elliot, D. 29, 76
Elliot, R. 29, 76
Ellis, J. 102, 105, 108

Ferguson, C.K. 135
Freire, P. 79, 81, 83, 84, 85, 87, 88, 89, 92
French, J.R.P.Jr. 15, 16

Galbraith, J.K. 28
Gibb, J.R. 79, 94
Glidewell, J.C. 128, 129
Gomolak, L. 74
Gorz, A. 66
Gouldner, A.W. 45
Grosch, H.R.J. 62

Harrison, K. 128

Harrison, R. 21
Hebden, J. 124
Hedberg, B. 51, 53
Herbst, P. 57
Hill, P. 58
Holloman, J.H. 31
Hoos, I. 73
Hoyt, K.B. 131
Huige, K. 106

Johnson, P.S. 40
Jones, G.N. 16
Jungk, R. 74

Kahn, R.L. 15, 21, 22
Katz, D. 15, 21, 22
Kellner, H. 86
Kelly, G. 81
Kelly, J. 135
King, D.C. 128, 129
Kling, R. 70
Koeppe, E. 73
Kornhauser, A. 73
Kuhn, T.S. 37

Langrish J. 33
Leminsky, G. 55
Lindholm, R. 59
Lippitt, G. 130

McGregor, D. 82, 113, 114, 118

MacMichael, D.C. 132
MacRae, G. 82
Mangham, I.L 130
Maslow, A.H. 81, 118
Mayo, E. 101
Mellor, K. 116
Mensch, G. 35
Mills, C.W. 82
Mouton, J.S. 113, 131
Morse, N. 15
Mott, P.E. 69
Mumford, E. 53

Norstedt, J. 59

Oddie, H. 128
Oshry, B. 129

Author Index

Ottaway, R.N. 22

Piaget, J. 103
Pirsig, R.H. 52
Post, J.E. 123
Preston, L.E. 123

Raithel, H. 74
Reimer, E. 15
Reubens, B.G. 132
Richardson, A. 13
Rogers, C.R. 15, 81, 136
Rose, S. 68
Rosenbrock, H. 69
Rosenburg, N. 32
Rosenstein, E. 123

Sanders, T.G. 84
Schelling, T.C. 129
Schiff, E. 114, 116
Schmookler, J. 32
Shaw, G. 124
Schutz, W. 21
Smith, A. 29
Smith, P.B. 128
Sorokin, P.A. 28
Speiser, A.P. 63
Spender, S. 17
Stalker, G. 45
Strauss, G. 123
Steele, F. 19
Steiner, C. 111
Sterling, T.D. 55
Stokes, D. 82

Taylor, F.W. 65, 71
Trist, E. 15, 132

Usher, A.P. 34
Utterback, C. 31

Walker, K.F. 93, 127, 128
Wallgren, K.R. 117
Weber, M. 45
Weddernburn, K.F. 83
Whisler, T. 45
Williamson, D.T.N. 49
Willmott, P. 83
Wilson, W. 78, 83, 91, 97
White, L. 25
Woolams, S. 106

Young, M. 83

Zemanek, H. 63, 73